DEBORAH FRANCES-WHITE

Deborah Frances-White is an award-winning writer and comedian, best known for her hit podcast *The Guilty Feminist*. The podcast has had over 150 million downloads and has been recorded live around the world at venues including the Royal Albert Hall, the London Palladium, Sydney Opera House and the Wellington Arena. Her book, *The Guilty Feminist*, is published by Virago Press at Hachette and is a *Sunday Times* bestseller. Her second book, *Six Conversations We're Scared to Have*, will also be published by Virago. Her BBC Radio 4 show, *Deborah Frances-White Rolls the Dice*, won the Writers' Guild Award for Best Radio Comedy and was followed by *Deborah Frances-White Introduces...* Her award-winning independent feature film, *Say My Name*, premiered in London's West End in 2019, and she has several scripted projects in development including *Bad Fairies* for Locksmith Animation with Warner Brothers. Her new feature film, *The Wishboard*, is in pre-production with Redwave Films.

Deborah's television credits as a comedian include *QI*, *Would I Lie to You?*, *Have I Got News for You*, *Mock the Week* and *Question Time*. She is a sought-after corporate speaker through her company The Spontaneity Shop and her Cambridge University TEDx Talk is available online. Deborah is an official ambassador for Choose Love and Amnesty International. She is currently the creative director of Amnesty's legacy brand *The Secret Policeman's Ball* and has directed and compered the *Secret Policeman's Tour* shows.

Deborah Frances-White

NEVER
HAVE I EVER

NICK HERN BOOKS
London
www.nickhernbooks.co.uk

A Nick Hern Book

Never Have I Ever first published as a paperback original in Great Britain in 2023 by Nick Hern Books Limited, The Glasshouse, 49a Goldhawk Road, London W12 8QP

Never Have I Ever © 2023 Deborah Frances-White

Deborah Frances-White has asserted her right to be identified as the author of this work

Cover image by Bob King Creative for Chichester Festival Theatre, photograph of Greg Wise, Susan Wokoma, Amit Shah and Alex Roach by Seamus Ryan

Designed and typeset by Nick Hern Books, London
Printed in Great Britain by Mimeo Ltd, Huntingdon, Cambridgeshire PE29 6XX

A CIP catalogue record for this book is available from the British Library

ISBN   978 1 83904 236 2

www.nickhernbooks.co.uk/environmental-policy

Never Have I Ever was first performed at the Minerva Theatre, Chichester, on 1 September 2023, with the following cast (in alphabetical order):

JACQ	Alex Roach
KAS	Amit Shah
TOBIN	Greg Wise
ADAEGO	Susan Wokoma

Director	Emma Butler
Designer	Frankie Bradshaw
Lighting Designer	Ryan Day
Sound Designer	Alexandra Faye Braithwaite
Movement Director	Chi-San Howard
Intimacy and Fight Director	Claire Llewellyn
	for RC-Annie Ltd
Casting Director	Lotte Hines CDG

Associate Director	Dubheasa Lanipekun
Dramaturg	malakaï sargeant
Additional Dramaturgy	Kate Bassett

Production Manager	Chris Hay
Costume Supervisor	Laura Rushton
Props Supervisor	Marcus Hall Props
Wigs, Hair and Make-up Supervisor	Shelley Gray

Company Stage Manager	Lou Ballard
Deputy Stage Manager	Olivia Roberts
Assistant Stage Manager	Georgia Dacey

Acknowledgements

I was highly privileged to have artists in our cast and creative team – both in development and in this first production – who contributed openly and generously about their identities and experiences and helped shape the script in extremely important ways. Without these collaborators and others who shared their insights on the characters, I would not have been able to write this play. I have also worked alongside many incredible co-hosts and guests of *The Guilty Feminist* (far too many to name!); I have learned so much from them, and my listeners, that has shaped my world view and I am indebted to them all.

Deep thanks to all the actors, dramaturgs and associates who worked on the play (named below) in development or production. And of course our very talented director and my incredibly generous collaborator who invited me to write this play for a development workshop at the Almeida Theatre – the wonderful Emma Butler.

Alex Roach
Amit Shah
Greg Wise
Susan Wokoma

James Lance
Stephen Mangan
Samuel West

Sian Clifford
Bethan Cullinane
Sara Pascoe
Milly Thomas

Nathaniel Curtis
David Mumeni
Akshay Shah

Sophie Duker

Kate Bassett
Hart Fargo
Yasmin Hasefji
Myah Jeffers
Dubheasa Lanipekun
Tom Salinsky
malakaï sargeant
Juliet Stevenson
Wesley Taylor

Huge thanks to everyone who worked on the first production and brought their talents to it and our excellent producers Francesca Moody and Eleanor Lloyd and their teams. Big thanks also to Daniel Evans and Justin Audibert and their incredible team who welcomed us to Chichester Festival Theatre and gave this text life.

D.F-W.

For Keith Johnstone, who we lost this year, aged ninety.
He discovered so much of what I know about story, play,
comedy, drama, improvisation and the magical invention of
pretend that is the theatre – and shared it generously all his life.

And for Patti Stiles who taught me Keith's discoveries, and
many of her own, with heart, patience and brilliance.

Without these two – there is no play.

Characters

JACQ, *thirty-something, white*
KAS, *thirty-something, British Asian*
ADAEGO, *thirty-something, British Nigerian*
TOBIN, *forty-something, white, English*
MAN IN A BASEBALL CAP

This text went to press before the end of rehearsals and so may differ slightly from the play as performed.

ACT ONE

Masada Restaurant, East London. Night.

Masada is Turkish for 'on the table' and an iconic Jewish symbol that means 'Never Surrender'. There are four counters with bar stools behind them and a food preparation and cooking station at each of them.

JACQ, *thirty-something, white, working class, jeans, T-shirt and an apron, is preparing a fabulous meal at just one station (with her back to the audience, facing the high stools where the diners would be sitting on the other side of the counter). She's dancing to Alicia Keys' 'If I Ain't Got You' as she works. Her movements are decisive, like a surgeon, and she has a lot of natural swagger in her hips and shoulders, and not just when she dances.*

JACQ *has natural authority. The kind you're born with. She'd make a great Mother Superior if she hadn't lost her faith in God and a great MP if she hadn't lost her faith in politics. She runs a restaurant because she'll never lose her faith in food.*

Just as she and the music build to a climax, A MAN IN A BASEBALL CAP *knocks on the glass door* (*upstage*) *and points at his watch.*

MAN IN A BASEBALL CAP (*through the glass*). What time do you open?

She smiles and points at the 'Closed' sign. He looks confused.

JACQ (*shouting through the glass*). We're closed tonight! Sorry!

MAN IN A BASEBALL CAP. Why are you in there making food then?

She kills the music with a remote.

JACQ (*shouting through the glass*). Um. Because it's my place, mate, and I can do what I want.

He stands there. She presses a button on the counter and shoots a jet of fire into the air. Restaurant pyrotechnics. The guy takes the hint and leaves.

(*Joshing to herself.*) Yeah, you better run!

She chops vegetables and turns the music back on and continues dancing and singing into a wooden spoon. A man's voice booms up from a hole in the floor.

KAS (*offstage*). Is the 2003 Château Pontet-Canet too much or not enough?

She kills the music again.

JACQ. What?

The man pops his head up through the hole, he has a bottle of wine in his hand.

It's JACQ's partner (both romantic and business), KAS, thirty-something, lower-middle-class, British Asian. He wears an open-neck, very white shirt. He's so eager to please you, it's a bit annoying. He's also a bit vain but in the kind of way where you look at him and think 'fair enough'.

He's shelved his dreams because JACQ's were so much better thought out than his and he spends more money on his hair than she knows or they can afford. He went on a course to learn about wine. All this makes him the perfect maître d' for Masada.

KAS. I was just saying, is the 2003 Château Pontet-Canet too much or not enough?

He waves the bottle at her.

We need to give them a good time and make them feel we appreciate them but we also need to make them not think we've spaffed their money up a wall.

JACQ. We do appreciate them. We haven't spaffed their money up a wall.

KAS. Yeah but what wine says that? I feel like a 2003 Pontet-Canet might say, 'We're drinking your losses' but the house red might say, 'Fuck you and the motorbike you rode in on.'

JACQ laughs.

JACQ. Christ. Drink every time he mentions his fucking 'Ducati Scrambler'.

KAS. Deal... But drink what?

He disappears momentarily and reappears with a case of wine. He heaves himself out of the hole and pops the manhole cover across.

Seriously. This is a sensitive evening. We've got to make them understand we did everything we could –

JACQ. – We did! Everything!

He lays the countertop as she prepares food.

KAS. And also... real talk?

JACQ. Real talk.

KAS. Okay, seriously, Jacq – I think we've just got to say they'll get their money back.

JACQ. Kas! It was an investment! Not a loan! His investment failed. So he doesn't get it back.

KAS. But –

JACQ. – But what about the other investors? You're not offering them a money-back guarantee.

KAS. They're not real people we have to have dinner with.

JACQ. It's one awkward meal!

KAS. But they're old friends and they helped us –

JACQ. – It's not 'they'! It was his money not hers! He made that clear. The patronising ponce.

KAS. Come on. I'm very fond of him. In a way.

JACQ. That should be on his business card. 'Tobin Blake. You're very fond of me – in a way.'

KAS *shrugs and it turns into a shudder.*

KAS. It's what my dad always said though, 'Borrow money. Lose a friend.'

JACQ. We didn't borrow money. He invested in a restaurant. We did a good job but we didn't turn a profit –

KAS *sighs as he polishes a glass.*

KAS. So are we using the word 'bankrupt' or not?

JACQ. Definitely not.

KAS. What are we saying then?

JACQ (*listing options*). Insolvent. Depleted resources. Winding up the shop. Closing-down sale.

KAS *picks up a pad from beside the register.*

KAS. Let me write these down. I feel like I'm just gonna blurt it out the second they come in. 'We're bankrupt!'

JACQ (*kissing him on the lips*). Let me do the talking. Just pour the wine and look pretty.

He polishes a glass, then stops and looks at her.

KAS. I'm going to miss doing this. With you.

There's a moment of quiet sadness between them.

JACQ. Relatable content.

KAS. Still. There'll be other dreams –

JACQ. – To fuck up.

KAS. If only we had fucked it up. At least we could get it right next time. You did everything brilliantly. And I did everything… well enough.

JACQ. You know what the accountant said, running a restaurant's a gamble. Most close down in a year. We've done really well to get to nearly two. We've smashed it really.

KAS *looks at her: Did we?*

(*So much for.*) All those predictions that people would continue to support local businesses after the lockdown.

KAS. Yeah, yeah.

JACQ *goes back to cooking.* KAS *puts down the glass he's polishing and turns to her. He slowly slides down onto one knee. She looks up – horrified.*

Will you marry me?

JACQ. Lol. No. We can't afford it.

KAS. Hackney Town Hall. Six friends. Honeymoon in Southend-on-Sea.

JACQ. We can't afford it.

KAS. Just the marriage licence and a Pret, then.

JACQ. Why?

KAS. I need something to look forward to.

JACQ. That's what *Bridgerton* is for.

JACQ *chops vegetables loudly.*

KAS. I'm serious.

JACQ. No you're not. What we have – works.

She chops faster.

Relationships should be based on a mutual fear of ageing alone and the understanding that there is a price to be paid for that.

She scrapes the veg into a pan.

And that price is the hundreds of irritating compromises we have to make every day.

KAS. See! Your wedding vows are writing themselves!

JACQ. Fuck it – open the posh stuff before the bailiffs take it away.

He opens the expensive wine.

(*Suddenly.*) Hey, there's no chance he already knows, is there?

KAS. Nah, I checked Google Docs again today. He's never opened one of the investor reports. I think he just really trusts us… Ughhh.

He crumbles at this idea and JACQ *sees her moment to grab the bottle, pour it into her glass and knock some back.*

Let it breathe!

JACQ (*looking at the label*). A wine like this is what's known as a 'fast breather'.

KAS (*sarcastically*). Ah, an asthmatic wine. They didn't mention those on my wine course.

He fills a glass and drinks too. She cuts a sliver of something sweet she's prepared and tries it. Yum.

JACQ. Well the baklava will be baller, even if the news is not.

KAS polishes the final glass and checks his hair in his phone camera.

KAS. Why do you think she stays with him?

JACQ. Married. It's very time-consuming to extricate yourself. Too much paperwork. Beware.

KAS. She's so regal though. I feel like she'd have people for paperwork. Maybe he's amazing in bed.

JACQ. Lol. I bet he explains to her *why* he's amazing in bed –

KAS. – Hah! Imagine the PowerPoint presentation…

(*Doing a parody of Tobin's posh voice.*) Note here the transition from Missionary Position to Reverse Banker.

JACQ laughs.

JACQ. On her hen night she described him as…

KAS *waits: Yes?*

(*Relishing it*.) Thorough.

KAS. OHHHHHHHHHHHHHHHHHHHHH WOW
OHHHHHHHHHHHHHHHHHHHHHHHHHHH!

JACQ *smiles and nods*.

JACQ. Thorough.

KAS (*to be fair to him*). Well, you don't want to be haphazard.

JACQ *stirs something that sizzles and shakes her head*.

JACQ. Yeah, well that was a decade ago. More! There's no way
they're still sleeping together on the reg.

KAS. We do!

JACQ. Sure. Just regular becomes less… regular. For everyone,
doesn't it?

KAS. That's what *Bridgerton* is for.

They kiss on the lips but it's like a high-five. KAS *waves at
the door*.

*Standing on the other side of the glass door are the couple
they've been waiting for*.

ADAEGO, *thirty-something, posh public-school accent
(specifically Wycombe Abbey), British Nigerian wearing a
truly fabulous purple jumpsuit. She doesn't wait for anyone to
include her. She's learned not to bother. She enters every room
like she's extremely welcome and central to events and it
absolutely works. She's a journalist, activist and broadcaster
at the heart of the social political action and the fizzing social
scene that goes with it. She thinks quickly and conceptually.
Her eyes takes in every detail of the room, like she's on* The
Generation Game *and will win everything she remembers*.

TOBIN, *forty-something, white, English, posh slightly matey
public-school accent (specifically Winchester but he's*

cultivated the odd, occasional, very mild London pronunciation or intonation to make himself more accessible), understated, very expensive clothes. He runs a sustainable hedge fund and is very pleased about it. He's got a sense of humour but he also truly believes in his own abilities in that way that some men do: he once put up his own shelves, so deep down he thinks, if necessary, he could probably land a plane or do a simple heart bypass with the right YouTube video.

They're both carrying motorbike helmets. ADAEGO also has an oversized tote bag.

KAS lets them in as he greets them. Shaking hands, taking coats and exchanging kisses.

Adaego!

ADAEGO. Kas! What an absolute treat to see you both!

KAS. Helloooooo, Tobin! How are you, mate?

TOBIN. Fine, mate. Good, yeah. Good.

TOBIN takes his coat off and goes on his phone.

ADAEGO (*to* JACQ). Hello, babe.

ADAEGO puts her helmet in her huge bag and pulls a perfect huge bunch of flowers out – like a magic trick. She gives JACQ the frankly inconvenient flowers and kisses her on the lips. JACQ passes the flowers to KAS without looking at them. He sorts the vase like a pro.

JACQ. Lovely-thanks-you-shouldn't-have.

ADAEGO. They're Queens of the Night. Reminded me of you.

KAS. Aw.

JACQ. Ridiculous. And you look amazing. Annoyingly so.

ADAEGO. I was speaking at a women's thing.

TOBIN (*without looking up from his phone*). She's always speaking at a women's thing.

ADAEGO (*melodramatically, with big joyful gestures*). Yes, I am, Tobin. Women in Business. Women in Broadcasting. Women of Colour in Journalism. We're rounded up on the basis of gender to feed at the same trough of canapés constantly. You must have to go to 'Women in Hospitality' things all the time, Jacq.

JACQ. Never been invited.

ADAEGO (*I will find and kill the organisers*). Well, that's outrageous! You mustn't be on the right WhatsApp groups!

TOBIN. Or the wrong ones.

JACQ. I'm fine.

ADAEGO (*urgent work*). No! I'll get you on them! I insist! They're a must-have for networking.

KAS. She'd love that.

JACQ. I wouldn't.

ADAEGO *looks at her.*

KAS. She means she doesn't have time.

ADAEGO. Always wonderful to have a man to interpret what one woman means when she's talking to another.

KAS *waves a white napkin in surrender –*

KAS. Sorry.

– as JACQ *reveals her first creation and* TOBIN *helps himself without being asked.*

JACQ. This is a deconstructed Turkish lahmacun.

(*Pointedly.*) Help yourself.

TOBIN (*thinks he's Michael McIntyre*). Deconstructed. I never understand why people pay more for something because no one's bothered to put it together.

TOBIN *makes 'delicious' noises as he eats.* JACQ *rolls her eyes at* KAS*: See what he's like?* KAS *jumps in quickly.*

KAS. What's everyone drinking?

TOBIN. We're on the old Ducati Scrambler tonight, so something soft for me.

TOBIN *pats his bike helmet on the counter.* KAS *and* JACQ *make eye contact and discreetly drink as per their agreement.*

KAS. Well, leave it here and get an Uber, mate! Pick up the bike tomorrow. Come on! We're raiding the wine cellar.

ADAEGO *puts both hands up, dramatically.*

ADAEGO. I'm not using Uber till they pay their drivers properly.

TOBIN. Not to mention protecting women from those underpaid drivers.

ADAEGO *approves and* TOBIN *nods indulgently in her direction.*

(*To* KAS.) Thus the Ducati!

KAS *and* JACQ *drink again.*

KAS (*to* TOBIN). Hey, I've got a new ethical cab app – all carbon-neutral women drivers. It's called Hail Mary.

KAS *looks at him: How 'bout it?* TOBIN *wavers.*

Come on. Have a drink! This won't be any fun at all if you're all sober and we're all smashed –

ADAEGO. – You're wrong! That's just how he likes his TED Talk audiences.

KAS *and* JACQ *laugh.* TOBIN *rolls his eyes.* KAS *pours them wine.*

I'm not joking!

(*Indicating* TOBIN.) This one's really doing a TEDx Talk.

KAS. What? Wow!

ADAEGO. It's about the only three things you can buy with money. Security, Status and Experience. You think there's things that fall outside of that but you're wrong. He'll do it for you tonight. Won't you, Tobin?

TOBIN *looks up from his phone.*

TOBIN. Er, I pulled out of the TEDx actually.

TOBIN *drinks the wine and throws his bike keys on the counter.*

ADAEGO. What? You didn't tell me that. Why?

TOBIN. I just think straight, white men have said enough for a while. It's someone else's turn to talk.

ADAEGO. Babe. You're so woke. In a good way, I mean. I fully love you.

She kisses him and strokes his arm affectionately.

(*To* KAS *and* JACQ.) Isn't he so woke? In a good way.

KAS. So woke.

JACQ. Very woke indeed.

TOBIN. Actually I don't think you're meant to say 'woke' unless you're African American. It's cultural appropriation.

ADAEGO *smiles tightly. The others busy themselves with pouring and busy work.*

ADAEGO. I think I can say it, darling.

TOBIN. I'm not sure because I was reading in *The New Yorker* that it's not a Black thing it's specifically about African Americans' relationship to law enforcement. Originates with the phrase, 'Stay woke to the po-lice.'

ADAEGO *smiles more tightly.*

ADAEGO. Oh. How interesting.

JACQ (*Jesus Christ*). So you're saying you're too woke to say 'woke'.

TOBIN. Yes.

ADAEGO *and* TOBIN *laugh and then kiss.*

KAS. So why aren't you doing the TED Talk though? I'd like to hear it. I don't know anyone who's done a TED Talk.

ADAEGO. I've done a TED Talk! About being a good ally! You said you watched it!

KAS. Oh yes. Sorry! It was great! Great!

JACQ laughs. TOBIN smiles and puts his phone down properly for the first time.

TOBIN. You know, they asked me and I thought about it and I just thought – that's fifteen minutes where a woman could be giving her perspective. And when I'm talking, I'm not learning because I already know everything I've got to say.

Everyone watches his lecture, mute.

So it's really a privilege in a way to listen and not speak for a while. Like being a student again.

JACQ. Yeah well –

TOBIN. – There are some incredible women of colour doing podcasts at the moment. There's Reni Eddo-Lodge, of course. There's the *NoShade* Podcast. And who's the one you introduced me to, darling?

ADAEGO. Oh, you mean –

TOBIN (*clicking his fingers and pointing at her*). – Anne-Marie Imafidon! She's incredible. Then there's the *Slay In Your Lane* girls.

ADAEGO and JACQ open their mouths to correct him – he sees and beats them to it –

Women, I should say! I'm actually thinking of starting a finance podcast where I exclusively interview women of colour who work in the city and get their take. Just let them talk about whatever they want.

JACQ rolls her eyes.

JACQ. Is it going to be called *A Word in Edgeways* with Tobin Blake?

Everyone laughs, including TOBIN.

TOBIN. I won't say another word.

ADAEGO. Now, that's a great name for a white man's podcast.

ADAEGO *and* JACQ *clink glasses*.

KAS. I don't think you should not do a TED Talk though. If
a white guy knows something I want to know, I don't want
him to be silenced.

JACQ (*laughing*). Silenced?   ADAEGO (*outraged*).
                                    Silenced?

TOBIN *gestures to* JACQ *and* ADAEGO: *Come on now*.

TOBIN. Let him talk.

ADAEGO. Sure! Talk away!

KAS. I'm just saying, right, we can all learn from each other.
And when I did my wine course…

TOBIN *and* ADAEGO *make eye contact, smile, clink and
drink.* JACQ *clocks it. Fuck. They've got their own drinking-
game joke. It's 'wine course'. The bastards.*

…The thing was that all the guys that knew this stuff there
were white and posh –

ADAEGO. Because of structural advantage –

KAS. Exactly, so, I don't want them hoarding the knowledge,
man.

JACQ. That's actually a good point.

ADAEGO. Well in that case, stop hoarding your knowledge on
how to run a successful restaurant and come to a 'Women in
Business' event! You should speak on the entrepreneurs one
they're doing! Shouldn't she, Tobin?

TOBIN. Defo!

ADAEGO. Let me ask Alice if there's a spot.

ADAEGO *gets on the WhatsApp.* JACQ *throws* KAS *a look
but he's busy topping up glasses and avoiding her gaze.*

JACQ. No please, Adaego, don't! I hate public speaking. I'd be terrible.

ADAEGO. Nonsense! It's only a panel! We can't ask for more representation and then refuse the spotlight.

TOBIN. Lean in and all that jazz.

ADAEGO (*helpfully updating*). No. We're not listening to Sheryl Sandburg any more, darling. She's only famous for working for a Batman villain.

ADAEGO gets a message and looks up from her phone, almost aroused by her immediate networking success.

Yes! She's thrilled! It's called 'Successful Entrepreneurs: How Women Are Walking the Walk and Cashing the Cheques.' I'm adding you to the group.

JACQ looks at KAS with 'We have to tell them' eyes.

(*To* TOBIN.) Isn't 'cashing the cheques' a bit old-fashioned? Who cashes cheques now? What about banking the cash?

TOBIN (*clicking his fingers and pointing at her*). Bacsing the cash!

ADAEGO. Good one, babe. I'll tell her.

TOBIN looks pleased. ADAEGO messages Alice and gets a WhatsApp back.

(*Furious as if this is a personal attack on* JACQ.) Oh godddd. Jacinta Allen's on the panel. Did you see her stupid bistro won a World Restaurant Award for Best Tweezer-Free Kitchen!

JACQ. I did.

She violently slams down a pot. KAS laughs ruefully.

TOBIN. What's a tweezer-free kitchen? Is that real or an *Onion* headline?

KAS. It's real as you are, mate.

JACQ. It means they just thump the food on a plate with their hands.

KAS. Like Neanderthals.

ADAEGO. Or the Bullingdon Club.

TOBIN. And they won an award for that, did they?

ADAEGO. Yes! You two should have won something. Your place is a gazillion times better. Didn't you enter?

JACQ. No. We did. We just didn't win.

KAS. We were longlisted for Original Thinking. Because of our in-dining chef-stations. But we didn't make the shortlist.

ADAEGO. Well that's out-fucking-rageous and typical of the injustice in the world.

TOBIN. Unspeakable. I shall alert Amnesty International.

She shoves him playfully.

ADAEGO. Sorry. I just can't bear Jacinta Allen. She's always telling me to have a baby. Like it's a pyramid scheme.

JACQ. Oh my god, yes! Did you get her Christmas card? She was lying in a pile of her children with her husband –

ADAEGO. And they were all naked!!   JACQ. And they were all naked!!

They all make 'arghhhh' noises.

JACQ. Why? Why would you do that?!

KAS (*outraged and delighted*). Who suggested it? And how did they get the kids to agree to it? One of them's nine!

ADAEGO. I think she thought it was whimsical.

JACQ. Remember that terrible poetry night she ran at uni. Her unrequited-love doggerel!

TOBIN. Come on. I'm fond of her… in a way.

KAS catches JACQ's eye. They hide their smiles.

KAS. I am too, Tobin.

ADAEGO. Of course you are, Kas! You were the one all her poems were about.

KAS *preens*.

KAS (*I'm sure that's true*). I'm sure that's not true.

ADAEGO *turns to* JACQ *with a sudden horrified thought*.

ADAEGO. Jacq! You're not going to have a baby, are you?

KAS. You never know.

JACQ *shakes her head behind his back: Nooooo. Definitely not*.

ADAEGO. You're my last child-free friend. And not to make your womb all about me but please don't. I need an ally.

TOBIN *is back on his phone*.

TOBIN. According to Instagram, Jacinta is opening a Tweezer-Free bistro in a second location.

ADAEGO. Would you two ever open a second location, Jacq?

JACQ *and* KAS *look at each other. Fuck*.

KAS. Shall we eat?

JACQ *hits the button on the side of the counter, fire shoots in the air. The lights snap to black. 'Yeah!' by Usher BLARES*.

When the lights come up, the music stops dead. Time's passed. More wine has been drunk and two courses have been eaten.

KAS *and* JACQ *have switched chairs*. TOBIN *and* ADAEGO *are staring at* JACQ *in shock*. KAS *has his head in his hands*.

ADAEGO. Bankrupt?!

TOBIN. Bankrupt?!

KAS. Bankrupt.

JACQ *looks daggers at* KAS.

ADAEGO. But how? The reviews are spectacular. And it's doing so well. And you were longlisted for Original Thinking!

JACQ. We were doing two sittings every evening – going great guns – but no wanker wanted to come for lunch and that was our margin done for.

KAS *feels sweaty and itchy.* TOBIN *almost pats his arm and then doesn't.*

TOBIN. I did say at the time that having to staff every counter might make it a bit untenable –

JACQ (*snapping*). It's the whole concept! It's the vision. It's not 'at the table' if it's 'in the kitchen', is it?

KAS (*to* ADAEGO). It was part of the post-lockdown pitch. Made people feel safe and in their own little space and so they could see how their food was prepared... but that wore off. Now they're all licking snakebite and black out of the gutter at two a.m. like the old days.

KAS *sighs.*

TOBIN. Well... What sad news.

KAS *can't stand it any longer.*

KAS. You'll get your money back, Tobin. We'll pay it all back, once we get on our feet –

JACQ. – Well, hold on –

TOBIN. – No! I won't hear of it. It wasn't a loan. It was an investment.

JACQ. See, I told him that's how it works, Tobin. I'm so sorry about it but –

TOBIN. – Don't be.

KAS. Yeah but I don't want to ruin the friendship –

TOBIN. Oh mate. I'd completely forgotten about it. It wasn't even a hundred grand, was it?

JACQ *gasps. That's galling. She looks to* KAS *and back to* TOBIN.

JACQ. It was a hundred and twenty.

TOBIN. A hundred, a hundred and twenty. We are are still in a very manageable ballpark.

JACQ *and* KAS *look at him. Really?*

Really. I know it seems like a lot of money, but really, guys, do not worry – in investment terms it's no more than a fun punt.

KAS *is so relieved.* JACQ *tries to swallow her rage.*

JACQ. Spare change for you, I'm sure.

TOBIN *drains his glass and shrugs magnanimously.*

TOBIN. Not exactly – but it meant I got to say I was the part-owner of a restaurant. I got to bring clients here and show off a bit! It paid for itself! Honestly.

ADAEGO *lunges for* JACQ *and grabs her in horror and over-the-top dramatic remorse at her faux pas.*

ADAEGO (*all about me*). Oh my god, babe! What have I done?! I've got to get you off that successful entrepreneurs' panel!!

She grabs her phone and messages. JACQ *drinks – FML.* KAS *pats* TOBIN*'s back uncomfortably.*

KAS. Tobin. Mate. Honestly. Thanks. You're making this easier than you need to.

JACQ *glares at* KAS *and* TOBIN.

TOBIN. Listen, you don't invest in restaurants to get rich.

KAS. True dat.

JACQ *can't stand it.*

JACQ (*to* TOBIN). So are you saying you guys were giving us charity?

ADAEGO *stares hard at her phone and texts to avoid eye contact.*

ADAEGO. Hey, it wasn't my money. This is exactly why I keep our finances separate.

JACQ. And what does that mean?

ADAEGO. I just don't like money. It makes things awkward.

JACQ *makes a noise like she's got a bone trapped in her throat.* KAS *puts his arm around her and makes a 'be nice' face.* TOBIN *claps his hands together to clear the air.*

TOBIN. Listen, if your wine cellar is going to be repossessed, let's see what kind of return on my investment we can get before it goes.

KAS *jumps up.*

KAS. My thoughts exactly.

KAS *wobbles down the ladder.* TOBIN *follows him.*

JACQ. Be careful! You're a bit smashed.

KAS *and* TOBIN *disappear and there's a crashing sound in the cellar.*

KAS *(offstage).* All good!

ADAEGO *hugs* JACQ *hard. They hold each other for ages.*

ADAEGO. Are we sure there isn't anything –

JACQ. – I'm sure.

ADAEGO. Let me look at the paperwork. In case there's a loophole with the lease or a way of extending credit you haven't thought of… Or a grant you're eligible for!

JACQ. Honestly, no. It's fine.

ADAEGO. At least let me look at your contracts – put my law degree to use for once. It'd make my mum so proud.

JACQ *laughs and disappears under a counter while* ADAEGO *picks at the food.*

JACQ. Shall I take a photo of you doing it and send it to her?

ADAEGO. Please!

JACQ *pops up with the paperwork.* ADAEGO *fishes in her oversized bag, puts on her funky reading glasses and starts going through the contracts and finances.*

KAS and TOBIN *come up the ladder, singing 'Toxic' by Britney Spears, tunelessly.*

KAS. Remember that, Jacq! Our first year at uni? They played this on a loop in the bar.

JACQ. I remember.

KAS and TOBIN *continue to sing together.*

TOBIN *comes up behind* ADAEGO *and puts his arms around her.*

TOBIN. You know I can't resist you in those glasses.

ADAEGO *doesn't move.*

ADAEGO *(flatly).* Try.

TOBIN. You working out a plan?

She makes a face. Not looking good.

Is the place still insured?

KAS. To the hilt.

TOBIN *opens a really old-looking bottle of wine in the rhythm of 'Toxic'.* KAS *looks at* TOBIN, *opening the wine as if he's the host, and is fascinated by his moxie.*

TOBIN *(so ebullient it's insensitive).* Then burn it down. Claim the insurance. Start again.

ADAEGO. Tobin! God! Have a bit of sensitivity for once.

JACQ. Aren't you meant to be 'Mr Sustainable'?

TOBIN. Jokes! You remember jokes, don't you?

KAS. Stop working! Come on! Have a drink!

He takes the wine from TOBIN *before he can pour and fills glasses…*

KAS and TOBIN *sing on.*

JACQ *gets dessert plates looking dispirited.*

JACQ. What a fucking disaster.

ADAEGO takes her glasses off and looks at JACQ.

ADAEGO. I'm so sorry, babe. I can't see anything obvious… Maybe something will come to me.

TOBIN. Look. Jacq. If it makes you feel any better, I honestly never expected to see that money again.

JACQ bangs dessert plates down on the counter. ADAEGO *puts her head in her hands.* KAS *disappears back down into the cellar to avoid trouble.*

JACQ. What?!

TOBIN. Most restaurants fail in the first year! You've done really well to get to almost two! Better than anyone expected!

JACQ. So you expected me to fail?

TOBIN. The way you set it up, with all these stations in an area like this, it was clearly a passion project, not a retirement plan.

JACQ. So you expected me to fail.

TOBIN. Well it's a bit of a moot point because…

JACQ. Because?

TOBIN. Because you did fail.

ADAEGO. Okay. That's probably enough now. This baklava looks to die for. What's in it?

JACQ (*to* ADAEGO). Pastry.

(*Without stopping, to* TOBIN.) I know you won't have heard of the cost of living crisis up on Mount O-Posh-Knob-Lympus but there are things you actually don't know, y'know –

TOBIN. – The thing is, Jacq, there are only really three things you can buy with money.

ADAEGO. Babe. I'm not sure this is the time –

TOBIN. – Status, security and experience.

ADAEGO *does the drinking game 'cheers' with herself, clinking a bottle of wine in one hand with her glass in the other and taking a sip.*

And this restaurant was a stab at all three. Status because it's a boutique concept place. And security because it was your attempt to make a living.

JACQ *mouths 'attempt', horrified.*

But in the end it turned out to be just one. An experience. And that's the most valuable thing you can buy with money, actually.

KAS *pops his head up with another case of wine – just in time to hear –*

JACQ (*to* TOBIN). You are such a knob... 'Actually'.

KAS. Jacq. Come on. Let's have a nice time.

JACQ. No. Someone's got to say it.

KAS. They really don't.

JACQ. You used to be so left-wing at uni, Tobin.

TOBIN. I'm still left-wing, Jacq.

ADAEGO. He is, Jacq. Mostly.

KAS *heaves himself out of the hole.*

KAS. How about a Malbec?

JACQ (*to* TOBIN). You are so money-driven now.

TOBIN *laughs.*

TOBIN. *I'm* money-driven? I could make so much more money if I weren't ethical. I am literally making the city a better place with sustainable hedge funds.

ADAEGO. To be fair, darling, that's like saying you're bringing Diversity and Inclusion to the Seventh Circle of Hell.

JACQ. Exactly! It's much harder to be a female demon. You're not trusted with a pitchfork.

ADAEGO. So few opportunities for torturing the souls of the damned. Never get any high-profile cases like Jimmy Savile or Hitler.

JACQ. 'Oh I get to torment Eva Braun, do I? You think we'd be a "good fit". I see.'

ADAEGO *and* JACQ *laugh. They clink glasses.*

TOBIN. Okay. Okay. I'm just saying until the 'glorious revolution when capitalism is dismantled', I'm just trying to make the world a slightly kinder, fairer place –

JACQ. – While making yourself richer –

TOBIN. – Well, there isn't any value in making myself poorer, Jacq – because then I crash out and leave finance for those who don't care about where their profits come from. I analyse carefully the impact of my investments on, for example, women and people of colour –

ADAEGO. – Women can be people of colour –

She points at herself.

TOBIN (*you've told me this before*). – Women and *men* of colour thank you, darling.

ADAEGO. And non-binary people –

TOBIN. – And non-binary people. Thank you, darling –

JACQ. – Well that's excellent obviously but you're still massively profiting from people who are in a very different position from you –

TOBIN. – But then I invest those profits ethically to support other fledgling local businesses on a micro level –

TOBIN *points around the restaurant. Case in point.*

You-win-some-you-lose-some – and on a macro level, we make sure we look at things like crop sustainability, carbon footprint, treatment of LGBTQ-plus people. The knock-on, long-term impact on Indigenous people –

JACQ. – That's very noble but there's no ethical consumption under capitalism –

TOBIN. – Yes there is – relatively.

KAS. I get what he's saying – while capitalism is doing its thing, there's no need to be a massive twat about it –

TOBIN. – Exactly, Kas.

JACQ. Is that the name of your hedge fund? There's No Need To Be A Massive Twat About It?

TOBIN. No. It's called Ethicapita.

JACQ. Ethicapita? That's such a paradox! Like LovelyHomicidia!

JACQ scoffs. ADAEGO makes a weird hand gesture, tries not to get involved and fails.

ADAEGO (*'she's kinda right' high-pitched noise*). Yeeeeaaaaa?

TOBIN (*to* JACQ). Okay. Well. Jacq. You'd know about paradoxes.

JACQ. What does that mean?

TOBIN. Nothing.

KAS shoots JACQ a pleading look that goes ignored.

JACQ. No. Say. You clearly want to.

TOBIN. You want investment when you want it.

JACQ. Yes, to make a local, family business, to make enough money to feed and house ourselves and to serve the community we're in. It's not for greed and hoarding wealth like you're one of those people on Marie Kondo who has rooms full of Christmas decorations they can't part with because they have a disorder – except instead of snow globes you don't need, it's cash you won't spend.

TOBIN fills his glass – ready to pontificate.

ADAEGO. It's always hard to know when enough is enough with Christmas decorations, money and, of course, wine.

ADAEGO *looks pointedly at* TOBIN *as he pours and drinks. He doesn't seem to notice.*

TOBIN. Look. Jacq. You want to go to the cashpoint and get money out. But you want no one running the financial district. Well my politics might have matured since uni but yours seem to still be very much at home in the student union.

KAS. Okay, let's calm down, shall we? We're having a lovely evening.

ADAEGO. Christ, Kas. Everything doesn't have to be lovely all the time. We're allowed to disagree.

JACQ. And it's not a lovely evening because we're declaring ourselves bankrupt to our most bankery friend.

TOBIN. Look, Jacq. I've tried to explain nicely. But the truth is I'm the most left-wing person here.

ADAEGO *falls back on a stool out of shock.*

ADAEGO. What?! Tobin! You're not more left-wing than me. I know. I live with you. Do you write for the *New Statesman*?

KAS *claps his hands and rubs them together.*

KAS. Enough of politics. Who's up for a game?

TOBIN *opens a box of chocolates.*

JACQ (*to* TOBIN). You are definitely not more left-wing than me. I haven't changed my values. I just don't feel I have a party to work with any more. Otherwise I'd be out delivering leaflets.

TOBIN. None of that matters, ladies.

TOBIN *takes a chocolate and offers one to* JACQ. *She looks at him – amazed – takes the whole box (which is hers!) and offers them around.*

JACQ. Ah! The real title of your podcast. *None of That Matters, Ladies.*

ADAEGO (*in a sing-song Radio 4 announcer voice*). Next on Radio 4, *Here's Where You're Wrong* with Tobin Blake.

TOBIN *rubs his hands on his thighs, annoyed.*

TOBIN. No. I'm more left-wing than anyone here because I actually pay for stuff. Public stuff. I fund things. Going bankrupt, Jacq, robs the public purse – it doesn't chip in.

JACQ. Well it's not a choice.

KAS. I brought Balderdash. Tobin? Our reigning champion!

TOBIN *ignores* KAS *and looks* JACQ *straight in the eye.*

TOBIN. But it is a choice. Because you chose to run a boutique concept restaurant and sell three-hundred-pound bottles of wine to those who can afford them. Knowing it was a massive risk.

ADAEGO. She was following her dream!

TOBIN. That doesn't make it liberal. It makes it selfish. She could have been a teacher or a nurse.

ADAEGO. A nurse?!

JACQ. Why couldn't I have been a doctor?!

KAS. You hate blood, Jacq, to be fair.

ADAEGO. No, come on. Why does she have to be a nurse or a doctor? Why do women have to be carers to be seen as left-wing – while posh white boys can run hedge funds and get rich?

TOBIN *turns to look at her.*

TOBIN. You forget, my love, that my tax last year will have personally paid for that new school round on Spark Street.

JACQ. I hope you've gone around and made the children say thank you.

ADAEGO. Perhaps they could name it after you. *Saint Tobin the Magnanimous Junior School for Grateful Children.*

KAS *gets out Balderdash and starts setting up the board.*

KAS. He's got a point. Someone's got to pay for things. At least he's not hoarding his money offshore.

TOBIN. Thank you, Kas.

JACQ. No. You don't get Brownie points for not stealing from society. Anyone who makes the kind of money you make is capitalising on the poor by definition.

TOBIN. I'm not because my investments are ethical.

KAS *shuffles the Balderdash cards.*

KAS. Well I think –

JACQ. – Maybe you should call your hedge fund Moral Relativism because with the excessive wealth you and your city-boy buddies –

TOBIN. – Not all boys. We employ a lot of women. And one 'he/they' actually –

JACQ *makes a face at the insensitivity of calling someone a 'he/they'.*

JACQ. I don't think you should call someone a – [he/they]

ADAEGO *stops* JACQ *from going further with a 'don't bother' face.*

ADAEGO. The first time Tobin was asked his pronouns, he unironically said, 'I and me'.

JACQ *laughs indulgently – that's almost adorable.*

JACQ. The point is, whoever 'he/they/you' all are – the money you're making from others for doing incredibly little – your kind of sustainability – is unsustainable.

ADAEGO. Ah! It's like you have a webcam in our house, Jacq, and can see all the arguments I've made over the years.

TOBIN *looks at* ADAEGO: *Oh really?*

KAS (*reading from a Balderdash card*). Is a carriwitchet A) An animal that hibernates twice a year?

TOBIN (*as if* KAS *hasn't spoken*). Well, you live with me, Adaego. And benefit from any investments I benefit from so –

ADAEGO. – Why do you think I keep our money separate?

KAS (*soldiering on*). B) An absurd question.

TOBIN (*to KAS over his shoulder*). That one.

KAS. A point to Tobin!

> KAS *writes it down, triumphant.*

TOBIN. And speaking of absurd questions, Adaego… Yours conveniently ignores that despite your separate pots of money, we live in Primrose Hill. And we got here… on a Ducati.

> KAS *knocks his drink back.* JACQ *drinks straight from the bottle.* ADAEGO *has caught on to their game and drinks too. Fuck it.*

ADAEGO. I'm an active, intersectional feminist. I'm at the coal face. You are not more left-wing than me and never have been.

TOBIN. You just said I was woke in a good way!

ADAEGO. For a straight white cis man!

> TOBIN *nods and rolls his eyes.*

TOBIN. Oh okay.

JACQ (*to TOBIN*). Oh you're woke-ier than thou – it doesn't make you a socialist.

KAS (*muttering*). I thought we weren't meant to say 'woke'.

JACQ. Shut up, Kas!

ADAEGO (*to TOBIN*). You just said it was time to listen to women!

TOBIN. To be fair, darling, anyone married to you has to do a lot of listening.

ADAEGO. Well, listen to this – I'm a broadcaster. I'm a journalist. I'm an activist. Both racial equality and body acceptance –

TOBIN. – Yes, darling. That all sounds great at dinner parties – you are an excellent identity politician – but what does any of it do? Who does it help? What does it change?

ADAEGO. Oh – well it's nice to know my life's work is meaningless to you –

TOBIN. Not meaningless, darling, of course. Just more of a really important… avatar that represents change more than makes it.

ADAEGO takes a deep breath and tries not to lose it.

ADAEGO. My influence personally got over five hundred people to come on the People's March Against Brexit.

TOBIN. You're making my point for me, now.

ADAEGO turns on him – furious.

ADAEGO. Sometimes I think you voted Leave.

TOBIN, JACQ and KAS all gasp. There's horrified chill at the table. TOBIN looks mortally wounded.

JACQ (*yikes*). Okay, that might be going too far.

ADAEGO looks at her phone ostentatiously as if to ignore him and then looks up, delighted.

ADAEGO (*to JACQ, BEST NEWS EVER!*). Oh my god! Alice says she's at the Groucho with Elizabeth Day right now! Would you like to do her *How to Fail* podcast instead? She's doing a 'real people' series and would adore to talk to someone who's actually gone bankrupt!

JACQ. No! Fuck off!

KAS. I'll do it.

Everyone turns to him.

As long as we all agree to change the subject.

JACQ. Far be it from you to nail your colours to the mast, Kas.

KAS. I don't have any colours.

JACQ. Or any masts! Exactly!

TOBIN. Never have I ever had such a fucking ungrateful response to writing off a debt.

JACQ. It's not a debt, it was an investment. You invested unwisely.

TOBIN. I certainly did.

KAS. This is why I said we should pay it back. You say it's not a debt and then it slips out.

ADAEGO *smiles widely and tops up everyone's wine.*

ADAEGO (*to* TOBIN). You said 'Never have I ever...'

TOBIN. What?

ADAEGO. 'Never have I ever...' Remember when we used to play that at uni?

KAS. Let's play!

TOBIN. I'm not playing a drinking game.

JACQ (*oh really?*). Kas, tell them about your wine course.

KAS. Three weeks in Tuscany. Intensive.

TOBIN *and* ADAEGO *drink.* JACQ *raises a glass to* TOBIN. *Okay. He's already playing one.* KAS *has caught on too.*

Alright! Alright! I learned all about wine!! Now, it's Never Have I Ever or Balderdash. That's my final offer.

TOBIN. Alright. But I want it on the record that I find it ridiculous.

ADAEGO. Let the record reflect!

KAS. It's like I'm right back at Rag Week. On the committee. Treasurer. Or whatever I was.

TOBIN. You were Secretary. I was Treasurer.

JACQ. Of course you were.

ADAEGO. I was Women's Officer. Christ! The endless complaints! What did you do, Jacq?

JACQ. I drank. I can taste the WKD now.

She makes a disgusted wriggly move with her whole body.

ADAEGO. Remember how Tobin always wore his coat inside – summer and winter?

She strokes him affectionately.

JACQ (*to* TOBIN). Lol. I used to wonder if you were naked under there.

KAS pours everyone a very expensive dessert wine in fresh glasses.

ADAEGO. He often was.

TOBIN. I thought it gave me the eccentric air of a Doctor of Economics before I got my doctorate.

ADAEGO. It made you look like Worzel Gummidge.

TOBIN. Thank you, darling.

ADAEGO. It's a compliment. You've got hotter.

KAS. Right. Get your motors running.

They pick up their glasses.

Never have I ever shagged my philosophy tutor in the quad after first-year exams.

He looks pointedly at JACQ.

JACQ. You're such a cunt, Kas.

KAS/ADAEGO/TOBIN. Drink!

JACQ. Fine but I want it on the record – she was smoking hot.

ADAEGO. And fired not long after, if I remember correctly.

TOBIN. Let the record reflect!

KAS/ADAEGO. Drink! Drink! Drink!

JACQ takes a gulp.

KAS/ADAEGO/TOBIN. Down in one! Down in one!

JACQ hits the pyro button as she downs the drink. The fire shoots up. The lights snap to black. 'Toxic' by Britney Spears blares for some time.

When the lights come up again, the music snaps off. Time has passed. The gang are all sprawled on different countertops, wearing an assortment of head boppers and those New Year's Eve glasses where the date goes round your eyes – but from different years.

JACQ. Never have I ever… joined the mile-high club.

ADAEGO *and* TOBIN *drink.*

KAS. Wow. When?

ADAEGO. We ended up going first class on Emirates. They have a shower.

KAS. Fairest possible play.

TOBIN *makes his best Sherlock Holmes face.*

TOBIN. Never have I ever… shoplifted…

JACQ *and* ADAEGO *both drink quickly.* TOBIN *and* KAS *look at them judgementally.*

KAS. What did you steal?

ADAEGO *looks sheepish.*

ADAEGO. CDs from HMV when I was fourteen.

JACQ. These jeans.

She laughs drunkenly and hits the pyrotechnic button on the counter. The flame shoots up.

The lights snap to black. 'Toxic' by Britney Spears blares again.

When the lights come up 'Toxic' is still playing and the gang are dancing. JACQ *and* ADAEGO *are on a countertop.* TOBIN *and* KAS *on the floor. They're really letting go, like they're back in the dodgiest nightclub in their uni town.*

KAS/ADAEGO/TOBIN/JACQ. DON'T YOU KNOW THAT YOU'RE TOXIC!!

TOBIN *hits the pyro button on the counter – the flame flies high.*

The lights snap to black. The music continues.

When the lights come back up – the music snaps off and the gang are all sitting on the same counter, side by side, facing the audience, with shot glasses.

KAS. Never have I ever gone down on someone in that little vestry bit in the uni library.

JACQ. That was with you! That's cheating.

KAS. Doesn't matter! You've still got to drink!

JACQ. Do I have to swallow?

KAS/ADAEGO. Heyo!

TOBIN *makes a 'cheers' gesture and knocks his shot back in one at the same time as* JACQ. *They all look at him: You what?*

JACQ. You?! In the library!? Tobin! I am sha-hocked!

KAS. Toban the man!

TOBIN. I did things when I was a fresher that none of you know about.

ADAEGO. Yeah! That's because we were in school uniform when you were a fresher!

JACQ. Junior school!!!

ADAEGO. Nursery school.

She laughs for ages. Then a bit more.

Oh my god. I'm so drunk.

She hits the pyro button and the fire flares up.

The lights snap to back. 'Toxic' blares. The lights come back up. 'Toxic' snaps off.

KAS *sings an original love song while* JACQ *accompanies him on a guitar.* ADAEGO *attempts to harmonise with 'la la las'.*

KAS *(singing)*.
Because it's easier not to try than to love –

As they sing, TOBIN *throws up in a bucket while leaning down over a bin under a counter and then pops back up and wipes his mouth with a cloth.*

TOBIN. Oh god. I feel so much better. Guys. I really recommend it.

The lights snap to black. 'Toxic' blares out. When the lights snap back on, the music underscores softly. TOBIN *and* ADAEGO *are now doing push-ups.*

KAS/JACQ. Nine, ten, eleven!

TOBIN *crashes out.* ADAEGO *keeps going and starts doing claps between each push-up.* KAS *and* JACQ *go wild, cheering.*

TOBIN. Oh alright now.

The lights snap to black. 'Toxic' blares.

The lights come up. 'Toxic' still plays.

They're dancing sexier this time. There's even some grinding. They all do tequila shots with salt. JACQ *and* ADAEGO *grind and have a little snog.* TOBIN *and* KAS *try not to look at each other.*

TOBIN *cuts a line of cocaine on the counter with a Balderdash card. He offers one to* KAS *who shakes his head: No thanks.*

KAS *hits the pyro button. The flame shoots up.*

The lights snap to black, the music continues to blare.

The lights come up – the music snaps off.

JACQ, ADAEGO *and* TOBIN *sit on stools behind the original counter. They've all got pint glasses of water. They're having more baklava.* KAS *pours a super-expensive whiskey.*

KAS. Never have you ever had a whiskey like this.

KAS *hands it round.*

Taste the fuck out of that.

They do. Wow. They make the right noises.

ADAEGO. Noice.

TOBIN *raises his glass: Cheers.*

TOBIN. Never have I ever had a threesome.

ADAEGO, JACQ *and* KAS *all drink.* TOBIN *looks skeptical – like Poirot sleuthing out the truth.*

Alright, I know you would've, Jacq, because you were all sort of bisexual at uni –

JACQ. – Still bisexual now, Tobin. Out and proud. Doesn't make me more likely to have a threesome though –

TOBIN. – Another in a series of moot points from you, it seems...

JACQ *rolls her eyes: Fine.* TOBIN *turns to* KAS *like Poirot.*

(*To* KAS.) But you, Kas? I don't know. You seem pretty vanilla.

KAS (*thanks*). Okay.

TOBIN (*to* ADAEGO). And you haven't, darling. I'd know! Have you?

TOBIN *turns to* KAS.

(*Scoffing, writing it off.*) No. I don't believe it. Are you telling me that all three of you have had a...

KAS, ADAEGO *and* JACQ *are very still and quiet.*

(*There's no way.*) All three of you...

They're stiller and quieter.

(*Hold on a minute.*) All three of you have had a threesome!?

(*Fuck no.*) Wait. No. Have you three had a threesome?

Suddenly they all move at once.

JACQ. Of course not.

KAS. Noooo.

ADAEGO. No! Don't be silly, babe. I haven't had a threesome. I drank accidentally.

TOBIN. No you didn't! You three have had a threesome. I can smell it.

JACQ. Oh. Well. No. Come on now!

TOBIN. You! Kas! You! You're so… nice. And weak.

KAS. Um, well, no.

TOBIN *pounds the counter.*

TOBIN. When did this happen?

ADAEGO *looks at the others. They've got to tell him.*

ADAEGO. Okay. Babe. I'll explain. But I need you not to freak out. Because it's not a whole big thing –

TOBIN. – I'll be the judge of that –

ADAEGO. – Alright. Calm down. Yes. We did have a threesome.

TOBIN. Oh god! I knew it!

ADAEGO. But it happened years ago when we were at uni. We did some MDMA one night at a party when we lived in that flat on Dove Street and everyone else went home and –

TOBIN. – We were together when you lived in Dove Street!!

KAS *and* JACQ *look at each other: Oh shit!*

ADAEGO. No! It was when you did that year abroad in France!

TOBIN. We were together when I did that year abroad in France!

ADAEGO. We had an understanding, didn't we?

TOBIN. Yes! An understanding that we'd be faithful! Like people with integrity.

ADAEGO (*rather high-pitched*). Did we?

TOBIN. Yes! I was back and forth all the time.

KAS. Mate. I'm sorry. I didn't realise –

TOBIN. – What?! That fucking my wife would ruin my life?

JACQ. Okay. That's a bit much. She wasn't your wife then. It was one night. We'd done drugs. We were a lot younger than you. We were in second year. You practically had a PhD.

TOBIN. How the fuck is that remotely relevant?!

JACQ (*reaching*). Because…

You'd done your experimenting, you know, all that going down on people in libraries as a fresher. You were in a different place.

TOBIN. France! I was in France! Working!

KAS. Honestly, I think it was just a 'time and place' thing. You had to be there.

TOBIN. Well, clearly I would have been there if I'd known you were all going to get naked and go hell-bent for leather on a rented sofa! This is seriously not okay.

ADAEGO. It isn't okay. And I apologise. Fully. But I was so young. I was so high.

KAS. So high.

JACQ. Really very high.

ADAEGO. And, babe – it was in another lifetime.

TOBIN. But you've carried it all this time and it's sat between us in our marriage – in this friendship. This secret. This terrible secret. Infecting us all.

JACQ (*placating*). Well, I've barely thought about it ever. So that's not true. Have you thought about it?

She looks at KAS *and* ADAEGO.

ADAEGO. Never.

KAS. I mean – occasionally – yeah obviously. But I always feel really bad afterwards.

TOBIN *looks at* KAS *with murderous eyes.* KAS *turns to* JACQ.

(*Quietly.*) We really should pay him back now, don't you think?

TOBIN. I don't want the money. I want…

The gang lean in – what does he want?

Justice.

ADAEGO. Okay. Nobody died.

TOBIN. I've been robbed. Of the truth.

JACQ (*evoking him saying 'stay woke to the po-lice'*). Well, I mean you can call the po-lice but –

TOBIN. – Do. Not. Mock. Me!

JACQ. Sorry. We are sorry.

ADAEGO. Really sorry. And if we could turn back time…

JACQ (*quietly evoking Cher*). If we could find a way.

TOBIN *makes a furious noise.* ADAEGO *and* KAS *glare at her: Stop making jokes FFS! It's not helping.*

TOBIN. Is my life just a joke to you?

JACQ. No. I'm sorry. You're absolutely right.

KAS. We'll make it up to you.

TOBIN. How? How will you make it up? What will you do? To make up for the fact that my marriage is a sham, built on a house of lies and sand?

ADAEGO. It isn't! Come on! Tobin! You know it isn't! It was one night and I didn't tell you because it was just something fun that happened –

TOBIN. Fun!?

ADAEGO. Not fun!!

JACQ. Not fun!

KAS. Not fun at all!

ADAEGO. Something inconsequential that happened, I meant. That was regrettable and over. And would have only hurt you. And we were in a way more casual thing back then –

TOBIN. – Apparently you were! I was committed. And you betrayed that commitment and lied for over a decade. Sorry isn't going to cut it.

KAS. What can we do? Tell us and we'll do it.

JACQ. Absolutely.

ADAEGO. Of course.

TOBIN. I want to have a threesome with the two of you!

He points wildly at ADAEGO *and* JACQ.

ADAEGO. What?! No! Are you fucking kidding?

JACQ. Absolutely not. Not if it was the last threesome on earth.

ADAEGO (*tiny bit offended*). Well okay now – that's a bit strong, Jacq. But yeah. No. Stop it!

KAS *puts his hand on* TOBIN*'s shoulder, kindly, like* TOBIN*'s having a breakdown.*

KAS. Come on, mate.

TOBIN *shrugs him off.*

TOBIN. No! That's the only thing that can make this better. It will level the playing field. And we will all be able to just get on again like nothing's happened.

KAS. I don't think we will, mate.

ADAEGO. Nothing *has* happened! Everything *is* the same! Why is this such a big deal to you?

TOBIN (*hysterically*). Because you slept with someone else! No! Not someone else! Some*two* else! Two other people! I was left out of the bed and the secret and everything. So the only way to keep our marriage and this friendship which I TREASURE by the way –

He points a finger at both JACQ *and* KAS.

– is to sleep with both of you.

He points a finger at both JACQ *and* ADAEGO.

ADAEGO. Why not him?

She looks at KAS.

KAS. What?!

TOBIN. What?!

ADAEGO. I slept with him and her. Surely you want the same.

TOBIN. No. I want the two women. No Kas.

ADAEGO. So you don't want what I had. You want what he had. Because he's the one you're really in competition with.

TOBIN. No – it's just that I am straight so… Look, the issue is one of infidelity. The only way to make this right is for parity. And equality of opportunity. Which is – when you think about it – the bedrock of socialism.

KAS *laughs.* JACQ *and* ADAEGO *explode at him: Come on! FFS!*

JACQ. Oh is this part of your 'most left-wing man in the room' pitch? Redistribution of vag.

TOBIN. It's about betrayal. And infidelity.

ADAEGO. No. This isn't about infidelity at all! You saw me kissing Jacq tonight and I didn't see you complaining.

JACQ *opens her arms wide.*

JACQ. Beware the woke white man.

TOBIN *is crying a bit with anger.* KAS *looks away: WTF?*

TOBIN. Don't say 'woke'! It's cultural – (*He struggles to say the next word because he's smashed and frustrated.*) approprop-iration!

ADAEGO. Oh, you don't get to say what people say if these are your morals. And a white man doesn't get to tell a Black woman what is or isn't cultural appropriation – ever. No. Obviously neither of us is going to engage in this ludicrous suggestion. We are all grown-ups, which is more than I can say for us when it happened at uni – and none of us will be engaging in sexual intercourse so that you can level some ridiculous score.

TOBIN. Fine. I've slept with you already. Loads. Thousands of times. It doesn't have to be you. Just you.

He turns to JACQ.

It'll be a deconstructed threesome.

A pause.

JACQ. Fuck off, Tobin. That's disgusting.

KAS. Mate, I think it might be time to go home. Sleep it off.

TOBIN. I'm owed something.

JACQ. No you're not. You might feel betrayed.

TOBIN. Might?!

JACQ. You can walk away from any relationship, any time – but you're not owed anything.

KAS stands up firmly.

KAS. Yeah. You're going too far, Tobin, and I'm going to have to ask you to leave.

TOBIN spins around – desperate. He stops and clicks his fingers in JACQ's *direction.*

TOBIN. How much to keep this restaurant open for two more years? If you don't make a penny.

JACQ stops.

JACQ. Why?

TOBIN. Because I'm asking.

JACQ. I don't know…

TOBIN. Ballpark it.

JACQ. Oh it would be a much 'less manageable ballpark',
Tobin.

(*Picking a number out of the air*.) Five hundred thousand
pounds.

He gets out his phone.

TOBIN. I can arrange to transfer that right now. I happen to be
quite liquid at the moment. It's sitting in an account. I'll
show you.

He pulls up an app with his bank accounts on them.

JACQ. What?

ADAEGO. Oh my god! Stop it!

JACQ puts her hands up over her head.

KAS. Fucking hell, man.

JACQ. Absolutely not.

TOBIN knows the 'absolutely' is wobbly.

TOBIN. Half a million quid. *Absolutely* not?

JACQ (*scoffing*). You're saying you'd give me half a million
pounds.

TOBIN. Yep.

JACQ. Is it an investment or a loan or –

ADAEGO. Jacq!?   KAS. Babe!

TOBIN takes his time.

TOBIN. It's a purchase.

JACQ stops. Oh fuck.

Two flames fly up from the counters. The lights snap to black.

End of Act One.

ACT TWO

'Let's Get It Started' by The Black Eyed Peas blares until the lights come up.

The gang are in exactly the same place. No time has passed.

TOBIN *cuts a line of coke with a fancy black credit card, gets out a small silver straw and does it off the counter.*

JACQ. Is that ethically sourced, sustainable cocaine then?

TOBIN *holds out the straw he's snorted it through –*

TOBIN. Anyone else?

KAS *comes up and frostily takes the silver straw. There's a palpable tension between the two men.*

ADAEGO. Be careful. Anyone could see in. And don't take your lead from Mr 'A small amount for personal use is a misdemeanor' over here – because I guarantee they'll assume you're his dealer, Kas.

KAS. It's very late. I think we're probably okay.

KAS *checks over his shoulder carefully, snorts it and splutters – clearly not used to it.*

JACQ. So, when you say 'purchase' –

ADAEGO. Jacq – even you joking about that is really fucking hurtful when he's clearly trying to punish me –

TOBIN. – When I say purchase, Jacq, I mean 'purchase'. A transaction. Both a merger and… an acquisition, if you like.

JACQ (*wow god fuck*). If I like?

JACQ *looks away.* ADAEGO *is jaw-dropped.*

ADAEGO. Why are you engaging with him, Jacq?

JACQ *makes a face*.

JACQ (*it's a lot of money*). I'm just asking questions…

ADAEGO. Why?

(*Turning to* TOBIN.) And why would you do this, Tobin? To our marriage? To our friendship?

TOBIN. What I'm offering is honest and upfront and all parties understand the terms. It's an ethical version of what you did.

KAS. Doesn't feel *very* ethical.

ADAEGO. Ethical? It's unspeakably cruel. I did something – understandable – when were in a much less committed –

TOBIN. – That's clear now!

ADAEGO. – We were boyfriend, girlfriend, not husband and wife! We were clubbing and going to the cinema! We hadn't built a home!

TOBIN. Oh, our white picket fence built of lies…

ADAEGO. Please stop this, Tobin. There's only so much longer that I can put it down to your usual, ugly, 'coke and booze' personality.

TOBIN.…But you can't 'stop' what you did to me 'cause it's in the rear-view mirror.

ADAEGO. Yes, so it's not real if you stop looking at it! It's a reflection!

TOBIN. I married you under false pretenses.

ADAEGO. If it had changed anything, I wouldn't have married you though.

TOBIN *stops*.

TOBIN. Are you denying I've been betrayed?

ADAEGO. Yes. It wasn't a betrayal really because I was too young to be in a committed relationship with a much older man.

TOBIN. Oh, I see! It's my fault for being older!

JACQ. You weren't just older. You were her supervisor, weren't you? This is maybe why you shouldn't shag your students.

TOBIN. She wasn't my student. I was her mentor.

JACQ. You mentored your way into her knickers, I remember. And then who wants to tell their mentor they did a load of mandy and that's why their essay is shit this week?

TOBIN. Don't try to make me the unethical one here! Michelle Obama was Barack's mentor when he was an intern.

JACQ *and* ADAEGO *explode with all sorts of noises.*

ADAEGO. So you're the Michelle Obama of the group, are you, Tobin?

TOBIN. Yes. In this capacity. I am.

JACQ. Wow. White men really do think they can do anything, don't they?

TOBIN. And that can fucking stop!

JACQ. What?

TOBIN. That 'white men' stuff.

ADAEGO. Are you seriously going to 'not all men' us when you're making this despicable offer?

KAS *makes a face.*

TOBIN. Yes! I am the wronged party!

I've been faithful and respectful since the day I met you! I'm one of the good ones! I'm not Harvey Weinstein! I'm not Louis C.K.! And I never have been. I respect women. Not just you! Women I don't have to respect!

ADAEGO *and* JACQ *balk.* KAS *is like: What now?*

JACQ. Like who?   ADAEGO. Who don't you
                                    'have to respect'?

TOBIN. Just random women. And now I walk into rooms and I feel the suspicion from them – at work, at events. I see the hashtags about people like me. And I've never misused my power. And how am I rewarded? All of you shagging and lying and laughing at me! I'm one of the good ones! And no one appreciates it!

JACQ. You know, a white lady put a cat in a bin a few years ago. Not once have I walked past a cat and thought 'Think yourself lucky, puss.'

TOBIN. But the cat doesn't make assumptions about you. Does it? The cat doesn't say, 'Oh a white lady! We know your sort!'

KAS. Hashtag Meow Too.

JACQ tries not to laugh. ADAEGO glares at him.

Just trying to lighten the mood and remind everyone how ridiculous this has gotten.

ADAEGO pulls at her hair in frustration.

ADAEGO. Tobin, my whole life has been people making assumptions about me. You think your humanity is being undermined by us not giving you respect? By people lumping you in with other less-virtuous white men?

TOBIN. I don't think. It is. I can feel it.

ADAEGO's eyes fire up.

ADAEGO. Okay. Okay. Remember going to that student drinks for Leaders of Tomorrow or whatever it was –

JACQ (*glaring at* TOBIN). – Corporate Cunts of the Future –

KAS snorts.

ADAEGO. – Exactly. Remember how the woman came forward and welcomed you and put a drink in your hand and I was right beside you! And she said I'd come in the wrong entrance and could she help me? Lovely she was. Until I realised she thought I was part of the catering staff and was trying to direct me out the back to collect my pinny.

She takes a moment.

And I want to get angry but I can't because then I'm the stereotype of the angry Black woman so I have to smile and make her feel better about her bigotry – her assuming my station in her world! And she keeps apologising. Fifty times I had to tell her that her racism was okay and I was fine. It wasn't and I wasn't! She was probably forty-five and I was nineteen. And you said to her, I remember –

She stops and takes her time.

'These things happen.'

TOBIN. I was just trying to smooth it over for you.

ADAEGO. No. You were right. These things do happen. If you're Black. You were trying to smooth it over for you and her! You could have stood up for me when I couldn't get angry.

TOBIN *looks away – guilty.*

(*To be fair.*) I worry about that less now. If people don't want to see angry Black women, they should stop doing things that make us so fucking angry.

TOBIN. To be fair, a white woman stood on my foot trying to get a selfie with you last week and she didn't even apologise –

ADAEGO. – Oh yeah, now *Guardian* readers make a beeline for me at book launches so they can show everyone they've got a new Black friend. It doesn't mean the 'collect your pinny' moments never happen. It's just now I never know why a white person is approaching at speed in my direction. It's racist roulette.

KAS *picks up some wine.*

KAS. Let's go back to drinking. That was more fun.

ADAEGO. We can't move on while this proposition is hanging in the air.

KAS. I don't think Tobin is serious.

JACQ. He is.

TOBIN. Deadly.

KAS *makes a face: Oh good.*

ADAEGO. How long have you been referred to as what you are
– a 'straight white man', Tobin? Four years? Five years?
You're sick of trying? Already? You're just not used to
trying. Trying is hard. Trying is relentless. You'd not last ten
minutes as a Black woman. Or a brown man. Tell him, Kas.

KAS *shakes his head.*

KAS. Nah, you're alright.

ADAEGO. What?!

KAS. I just don't think it's the moment for me to be lecturing
Tobin. Now shall we have a white wine or a wine of colour?

He busies himself with bottles.

ADAEGO. I'm not asking you to lecture him. I'm asking you to
explain what assumptions are made about you. How you're
treated differently. Searched at airports.

KAS. We don't get abroad much, with the restaurant.

JACQ. Oh god.

KAS. Honestly? I just keep my head down and try not to
engage. We all have issues, don't we? –

ADAEGO. – Kas, are you serious? –

KAS. – It's more that I feel a bit responsible and don't want to
rub salt into the… threesome…

JACQ. Please stop talking forever.

TOBIN. No. That's very good of you, Kas. It hasn't done a
thing to make it all better. But at least someone sees that I've
been betrayed.

He glares at ADAEGO.

KAS. Look. If it helps, Tobin… Adaego didn't start it… that
night…

TOBIN *turns to him. Very interested.*

TOBIN. Oh yes. Who did? Let's have some details.

JACQ. Kas! Stop!

KAS. I just want them not to break up on our account, Jacq. I was worried we'd lost his money and now – y'know –

TOBIN. Go on. I'm intrigued. How did this tale of rabid bacchanalia begin?

JACQ. Fine. I started it. I fancied Adaego. I thought you were too old for her and I didn't like you.

TOBIN. Yes you did!

JACQ. Surely, as much as you believe yourself to be an expert on every fucking thing, you do not imagine yourself to be the authority on whether I like you.

KAS. She's very fond of you, really.

JACQ. I'm not, Kas. That's you. That's what you say about him. I say, 'I don't like him.'

TOBIN (*huffy*). Well, I always thought we got on very well.

ADAEGO. Can men stop telling women what they think for one fucking minute!

JACQ. Kas and I were just flatmates then. It was Adaego I liked and I made the move.

TOBIN (*to* KAS). So why did you get involved?

KAS. I think it was the drugs. (*His pathological truth-telling disorder compels him to add:*) Also the fact that my super-hot flatmates were up for sex with me.

JACQ. Kas!

KAS. Yep! Good! Right! Stop!

JACQ (*to* TOBIN). Are you happy now? It wasn't her. It was me. I betrayed you.

ADAEGO (*to* TOBIN). There you go. Jacq seduced me. I was... less experienced.

JACQ *looks at her. A bit taken aback and hurt.*

TOBIN (*to* ADAEGO). You could have said no.

JACQ. Well if it makes you feel any better, she was just experimenting to say she'd done it once.

ADAEGO. Excuse me?

JACQ. The next day you instituted a 'never speak of it again' policy, Adaego.

ADAEGO. Because I had a boyfriend!

TOBIN. So you didn't think we had 'an arrangement'! The dominoes begin to fall.

ADAEGO *bites her lip: Damn.*

JACQ (*to* ADAEGO). Then why did you do it? You knew I had feelings for you. You knew I was into you. You could have experimented with someone else.

ADAEGO. No one else was offering. It just happened.

JACQ. So I was just adjacent. I see. And my feelings were… irrelevant.

TOBIN. How has this become about your feelings?! You admit you were trying to get my girlfriend to leave me for you! You admit that! You admit it wasn't a bit of high experimentation gone wrong – that it was a calculated move to steal her away!

ADAEGO. I cannot be stolen. I am not your property.

That hangs in the air for a long time.

TOBIN (*to* ADAEGO). I'm sorry.

ADAEGO. You should all be sorry.

JACQ. Well, so should you. Because you fucked me up that year.

I'll be honest, Adaego. I think you're the reason I'm not in a long-term relationship with a woman.

KAS *looks around: What?*

KAS. I thought I was the reason you weren't in a long-term relationship with a woman.

JACQ. Yes but I probably wouldn't have got together with you. Not permanently. I'd slept with men at that point – but I'd only had girlfriends. I think that experience with Adaego was so hurtful, it made me frightened of being with a woman romantically for a while –

ADAEGO (*to herself mostly*). – Because men are famously never hurtful –

JACQ (*to* KAS). And that's when you and I got it together for the first time.

KAS. Well, that's nice to know. Really excellent to have clarity.

ADAEGO *scoffs*.

ADAEGO. Come the fuck on!

JACQ. What?!

ADAEGO. Are you honestly saying I'm the reason you're not a lesbian, Jacq?

JACQ. No. The reason I'm not a lesbian, is because I'm bisexual. The reason I'm not in a same-sex relationship possibly has its origins –

KAS. – Wow, so this is my origin story now. I had no idea I needed one. Perhaps I'm a superhero who's been bitten by a radioactive bisexual –

JACQ (*talking over him, to* ADAEGO). – Possibly had its origins in the way you, a straight woman, played with my feelings so she could drink when someone said 'Never have I ever had a threesome' and seem like a more interesting person.

ADAEGO. Wow. Well, just wow. Well honestly the reason I didn't want to talk about it ever was that you made me feel fetishised. I believe you said on the night, and I quote, 'You're the first Black girl I've kissed.'

JACQ. Because you were! I wasn't saying it to –

ADAEGO. – Make me feel exotic? Less of a sexual being and more of a scene in a movie?

JACQ. Look, as a straight woman you may not realise –

ADAEGO. – Why are you assuming I'm straight, when clearly I had sex with you? You can't play that card. I'm a queer Black woman.

TOBIN. First I've heard of it!

JACQ. Bullshit! If you were a queer Black woman you'd have a podcast about it! Name one other woman you've done more than kiss.

KAS *puts his head into his hands.*

KAS. Please don't.

TOBIN. Yes do! Get them all out onto the table.

JACQ. And don't say Petra Baker because I know that was above the waist.

(*To* TOBIN.) And before your time!

ADAEGO (*to* JACQ). As I believe you said to that man in that pub in Shoreditch that time, 'I don't have to present my dating history to you to prove I'm bisexual.'

JACQ. Well by that logic, I'm not a white woman.

ADAEGO. Oh! Are you Rachel Dolezal now, are you?

JACQ. No. My grandmother was a quarter Turkish and a quarter Jewish. I'm sure you didn't listen when I told you but that's why the restaurant is called Masada. In Turkish it means 'at the table' and to some Jewish people the Masada story has great meaning. It's the sacred site of the ultimate resistance against power. It means 'never surrender'.

KAS. Which is a bit ironic now we're voluntarily declaring bankruptcy, to be honest.

ADAEGO. So you're one-sixteenth Jewish and one-sixteenth Turkish? And you're saying you're not white? Seriously? That –

She points at the word 'Masada' on the glass door.

– is a meaningful use of the phrase 'cultural appropriation'. One sixteenth! Come on!

JACQ. I was very close to my nonna! I can call my restaurant after the way she taught me to cook, thank you!

ADAEGO. Fine! But you're not not-white!

JACQ. I'm as not-white as you are queer. And if you won't admit that, go fuck yourself.

ADAEGO pushes JACQ's shoulder. JACQ pushes ADAEGO's drink over her. ADAEGO slaps JACQ's face. JACQ gasps, stops, then turns to TOBIN.

For five hundred thousand pounds you only get to go down on me.

TOBIN. What do I get for the seven-fifty?

JACQ. The same.

TOBIN. Five hundred thousand it is, then.

The flame shoots up. 'Let's Get It Started' blares as the lights snap off.

The lights come up on JACQ and ADAEGO standing opposite each other in the wine cellar – floor-to-ceiling wine racks surround them on three sides. We find them right in the middle of it. Furious as fuck.

JACQ. Your marriage is over anyway, isn't it?! If this is what he's offering. And the friendship certainly is. So why shouldn't I save something?! Save myself?! At least!

ADAEGO. Because it's disgusting. You won't just be bankrupt. You'll be morally bankrupt.

JACQ. I listened to you talk for forty minutes on a podcast this week on 'the rights of the sex worker'!

ADAEGO. Oh come the fuck on –

JACQ *gets her phone out of her pocket.*

JACQ. I've got it here –

She starts scrolling through her phone apps.

ADAEGO. No. That's not relevant.

JACQ. It's all that's relevant!

She brings up the podcast and plays it.

PODCAST PRESENTER (*from phone*). Welcome to *All About Eve* with Annie Felder. Now, before I introduce today's guest I wanted to recommend Hello Fresh, a great option for the woman on the go –

JACQ *scrolls forward.*

JACQ. Hold on.

ADAEGO. Are we seriously going to listen to a fucking podcast right now?!

JACQ*'s pulling up a few words here and there until* –

JACQ. Here!

ADAEGO'S VOICE (*from podcast on phone*). Under a capitalist society women's bodies are commodified anyway and we have the right to package and sell them as we see fit – and that right needs to be protected. Whether it be OnlyFans or providing in-person sexual services in which women take control –

PODCAST PRESENTER (*from phone*). – But surely the point is, only women in extreme hardship would pursue actual sex work –

ADAEGO'S VOICE (*interrupting*). – No, Annie, society needs to understand that any woman, any time, can place a premium on financial liberation and independence, which are noble goals.

JACQ *stops the podcast.*

JACQ. Any woman! Any time! Noble goals!

ADAEGO *is nonplussed.*

ADAEGO. That's very different from this.

JACQ. How?

ADAEGO (*quietly*). Because it's… personal…

JACQ. Exactly. Your politics are theoretical and always have been.

JACQ *looks at her: Checkmate.*

ADAEGO. You know what's not theoretical? My friendship. I care about you, Jacq. How can you not care about me?

ADAEGO *cries a bit.* JACQ *stops. What is she doing? She comes over, tries to put her arm around her. Fails. Goes for a pat on the arm.*

JACQ. Adaego. I'm… sorry.

ADAEGO *shrugs her off.*

Just when you said you were queer it really felt –

ADAEGO. – Fine. I'm straight. I'm not narrow.

JACQ *shakes her head.*

JACQ. No. Actually it's not for me to say who you are or to force you to say you're not anything. This got out of hand – and he should never have offered it and I shouldn't have… even for a second… It's just so much money.

ADAEGO. How is the amount relevant?

JACQ. You've always had money or you wouldn't ask that. You don't know what it feels like to be poor. You've never even been broke.

ADAEGO. I was broke after uni when I was freelancing –

JACQ. – No. You could always call your mum even when you didn't – and that's 'outta cash' it's not broke.

JACQ *puts her hands over her face.*

ADAEGO. Money really really doesn't make you –

JACQ *puts her hand up towards* ADAEGO*'s mouth.*

JACQ. – Don't say it! Do not say it! I've never had more than my overdraft in the bank. You went to the right school. You've had sex in a shower on a plane. Never mind the sex even – you had a shower on a plane!

ADAEGO. Okay but that part really is just nonsense, Jacq –

JACQ. – To you! Nonsense to you. You said you find money awkward tonight. It's fucking galling!

ADAEGO. You find it galling that a Black woman has money?

JACQ (*outraged*). I didn't say that! I'm saying you don't know what it is to be raised on a stabby council estate! To be working class –

ADAEGO. – You have a degree. You have a boutique restaurant. Nothing boutique is working class –

JACQ. Working-class people are allowed to do things, you know! We are allowed to have ambition.

ADAEGO. And you've got it! We're standing in your wine cellar!

JACQ. But it was all temporary and that's not about money. Rich people have three failed restaurants before they have one successful one. You need chances… It's Jacinta Allen getting in with the right middle-class critics and tweezer-free fucking judges.

ADAEGO. You could do that! You don't want to be on the right WhatsApp groups! On the right panels!

JACQ. I don't fit in there! I never have! They make me feel like some poor cousin in a hand-me-down… wine cellar. You sail through the door like you're the ringmaster!

ADAEGO. Look at me! I have to! I can't creep into rooms apologising – because someone throws a pinny at me! I can't get away with that shit! I learned to come into parties like I'm Oprah handing out free cars, years ago.

JACQ. Whatever you're doing, it's working! I trained as a chef and I had to flip burgers for years. I couldn't get arrested.

ADAEGO *stops and laughs ruefully.*

ADAEGO. Why do white people brag about that so much?

JACQ. Not literally.

ADAEGO. No, but it's your favourite fun phrase when everything's not going your way. 'I couldn't get arrested.' The thing is you would actually have to work very hard to get arrested, Jacq.

JACQ. Actually, I did get arrested for stealing tampons when I was fourteen. That's what I really shoplifted.

ADAEGO. So take Tobin's money. You're a white working-class woman raised in poverty. What's a quick fix? Take this cheque. I'm a Black woman raised in a world of racism. What's a quick fix for that?… There's no cheque.

JACQ *stops. Yes. She knows that. There's a long pause.*

JACQ. Adaego. Of course I'm not going to take his money. And I'm not going to let him touch me. I'd never do that to you. Never.

The women look at each other. The lights go out and the Black Eyed Peas' 'Let's Get It Started' continues as the lights come up on the restaurant. TOBIN *does another line of coke.* KAS *judges him.*

KAS. She's not going to take your money, mate.

TOBIN. I believe that is what both she and you believe.

KAS. Well surely I know her and she knows her – better than you know her.

TOBIN. I know people. I've worked in finance long enough to know that once the seller has entertained the idea of selling, they're just contemplating the price.

KAS. You're a bit of a cunt. Do you know that?

TOBIN. You've never met an actual cunt.

KAS. Oh. I think I have.

TOBIN. Work in private wealth management for ten years and get back to me.

KAS. No thanks.

TOBIN. No one here tonight is powerless. The problem with offering money for services occurs when someone is vulnerable. Not when someone is greedy. I am not covering anything up like Adaego did. Like you all did. And I am not taking advantage of anyone.

KAS. Jacq has integrity. Your offer has none. She's never gonna do it.

TOBIN. She will certainly come up here and claim that is the case. And then highly probably find a good, solid reason… to change her mind.

JACQ *comes up from the basement alone and looks at* TOBIN *and* KAS.

JACQ. I'm definitely not doing it.

TOBIN (*to* KAS). I know people.

JACQ *looks at* KAS. *What?*

KAS *hits the flame. 'Let's Get It Started' continues. The lights snap to black and come back up on the wine cellar as the music snaps off.* ADAEGO *and* TOBIN *face each other, in the middle of a row.*

ADAEGO. You still work with Paul.

TOBIN. What?

ADAEGO. After everything Kay told you about him. Nothing changed. When push comes to shove – you don't care who he's pushed and shoved.

TOBIN. If he'd done it, you know I'd have nothing to do with him –

ADAEGO. – How the fuck do you know he didn't –

TOBIN. Because she's clinically batshit. And I would know if –

ADAEGO. – You weren't there and you know nothing –

TOBIN. – He was my best man!

ADAEGO. And you were his. And look what you're doing tonight. I bet if someone told him this he'd say, 'Tobin would never.' 'There must be more to it.' 'Adaego must have gone insane.' Right?

TOBIN *looks ashamed for a second.*

Please, Tobin. Just why? Why *are* you doing this?! It can't be the threesome. This is too big a response for me shagging someone in *uni* –

TOBIN. – Not someone. Them! Our two most inept, needy friends.

ADAEGO. Oh so you don't feel superior to them any more. Is that it?

TOBIN. You're telling me if it were the other way around, you'd not find a way to settle the score?

ADAEGO. Not like this! The entitlement you have. You're so overflowing with privilege you walked away from a TED Talk to make yourself look good!

TOBIN. No I didn't.

ADAEGO. You did it to boast that you left your leftovers for people like me. 'I'm donating my fifteen minutes of internet fame to charity. I'll gift it from on high to a little woman of colour to say her piece'–

TOBIN. – That's not how it happened.

ADAEGO. Well how did it happen? Did they congratulate you on your humility? Do you get Nectar Points towards a knighthood?

TOBIN. I didn't get offered the TED Talk. Okay?

ADAEGO. What?

TOBIN. I told you I had it because Alan said he'd recommend me and I thought that meant I had it.

ADAEGO. Why the fuck would a recommendation mean you had it? Oh... because it always has before now –

TOBIN. – But they said – and I quote – 'We are looking for a woman or a person of colour to fill the slot.'

ADAEGO (*correcting him*). A woman can be a person of colour.

TOBIN (*it's like their old routine but with venom replacing the affection*). Thank you, darling.

ADAEGO. They just wanted –

TOBIN. – They wanted you. Or him. Or her.

He gestures up through the floor.

ADAEGO. God. It must be really annoying, Tobin. Hundreds of years of white male supremacy and you were born five years too late. (*A beat.*) Except you weren't. You've got everything! You just lost a TEDx Talk you never even had – you only thought you had because every other time in your life you wanted something – you fell out of bed onto it!

TOBIN. Whatever society has bequeathed to me or robbed from you – in our relationship – which I believe is a more or less egalitarian space – you robbed the truth from me. You accepted my proposal under false pretenses. I never would have made it if I'd known you'd slept with him while I was lying chaste in my Paris bed.

ADAEGO. Chaste in your Paris bed? You're not a Victorian heroine, dying of consumption. And just because you didn't fuck around doesn't mean you're allowed to settle some score by –

TOBIN. – It's for my mental equilibrium. If I were a woman I'd be allowed to call it 'self-care'.

ADAEGO. Self-care?!

TOBIN. Isn't that what women say now when they want to cancel at short notice without apology?

He looks at her: Hmmm?

ADAEGO. Well, this has been brewing for a while –

TOBIN. – Men's mental health is an epidemic, isn't it? What I'm proposing is entirely for my peace of mind.

ADAEGO. Don't kid yourself with this obscene arrangement, Tobin. You're not trying to buy security.

TOBIN. I'm aware I'm buying… experience.

ADAEGO. No, this purchase would be a hundred per cent status.

They look at each other for a while.

TOBIN. I can spend my money how I want.

ADAEGO. Fuck you, Tobin. Why would you do this?! Pride!? Ego?! It's something! What is it? What is it? What is it?! What is it?? What –

TOBIN (*exploding*). It's the whole last five years! Every time we go out I'm the butt of your jokes. 'So woke' with a pat on the head. Or not woke enough. Every fucking thing I say is written off because I am the opinion holder! And I never sold you out. When people were dismissive of you, I didn't mock you. I let you speak –

ADAEGO. – Let me!?

TOBIN. You know what I mean! I'm your husband. And you stand there and side with her again and again, like I'm nothing and no one.

ADAEGO *softens*.

ADAEGO. You're not nothing. You're not no one. I used to think you were everything. Sometimes you were… something else. But, Tobin, you're still my someone.

They look at each other.

I'm so tired… So tired.

TOBIN *goes to touch her, to comfort her – and she recoils. It riles him.*

TOBIN. Just tell me why I'm so publicly risible. The things that used to be the pillars of my confidence – my certainty, my education, my opinions – now seem to be demerit points. It's all happened so fast. For you to advance, do my sort need to be humiliated?

ADAEGO. Of course not –   TOBIN. And yet –

TOBIN *looks at her.*

ADAEGO. I'm sorry. You should've said you were struggling. I would've stopped. I will stop. But what cannot stop is women standing together now – the way men always have before. We have to! We waited to be listened to. We waited to be taken seriously. We waited to be let in. No one fucking listened. So now we are taking control of the means of the broadcast. So yeah, I'm not able to placate you all the time any more as much as I love you. Women have to be an army, because we're at war.

TOBIN. Well, let's see if your platoon upstairs is going to fall into line or take the big payday.

The lights snap to black. The Ruth Roubelle cover of 'Seven Nation Army' by The White Stripes pulses.

When the lights come up and the music snaps off, all four of them are standing in the restaurant.

Each one is at a different counter. It's like a Reservoir Dogs-*style Mexican stand-off but there are no guns…*

So we are agreed, no one wants the money. To be clear, as soon as I walk out the door, the offer is rescinded.

ADAEGO. We are agreed. Jacq?

She looks at JACQ.

JACQ. Agreed.

TOBIN. Kas?

KAS. Hey. Mate. It's not my body. It's not my decision.

TOBIN. So you're open to the money?

KAS. I didn't say that. I don't want the money. I want Jacq to be happy and know she's made the decision herself. I don't want her to carry any resentment away tonight because that will have… consequences.

TOBIN. So we are not agreed I should leave just yet.

TOBIN *looks pointedly at* JACQ, *who says nothing.*

ADAEGO. For Christ's sake, Kas! Jacq's already said no. It's okay for you to get off the fence, say you agree, and let us all get out of here.

KAS. It's her body. It's got to be entirely her decision. I shouldn't have a vote. It's just important to me she's not bullied into anything.

ADAEGO. You're not doing feminism any favours by giving him what he wants, y'know. It's hardly bullying to say, 'I'd rather you didn't let him perform cunnilingus on you, if that's alright with you.'

KAS. I didn't mean bullying from me.

He looks at her pointedly.

ADAEGO. Me?! I'm a bully? Because I don't want her to – What?! Oh, am I a bully because I've got an opinion? Is that not what a 'respectable immigrant' does? I see. Well, while *you* perform 'the dance of the amenable brown man' for the white people, you leave the work of the fight – this fight – all the fights – for people like me. How convenient. You get the outcome you want but I'm the troublemaker.

KAS. No, it's –

ADAEGO. – It wouldn't kill you to speak up and tell the rich white man you're obviously scared of, what you really mean, *Kasim*.

KAS *spins around and something comes over him. Comes out of him. From deep inside.*

KAS. Oh fuck right off, Adaego.

Everyone takes a breath. This is new from KAS.

ADAEGO. What?!

KAS (*calling back what* JACQ *said to* TOBIN). Is this podcast called *A Word in Edgeways with Adaego Blake*? Or are only brown people who *agree with you* allowed to respond?

JACQ. Don't tell her to fuck off.

TOBIN (*enjoying it*). Here we fucking go.

KAS. No! All of you.

(*Pointing at* TOBIN.) Especially you! Shut the fuck up! You want me to nail my colours to the mast, Jacq? Pass me a hammer.

JACQ *goes to respond but he ploughs through.*

You want me to stand up for myself, Adaego? So I'm gonna! I'm gonna talk. No! I'm gonna *TED Talk*! Where's my platform?

He drags a stepladder over from a behind a counter and walks up a couple of steps, like he's at Speakers' Corner.

JACQ. Come down, Kas.

KAS *waves her to shush.*

KAS. I'm on the ladder of truth. In vino very Kas.

JACQ. Oh god.

TOBIN *and* ADAEGO *are speechless.*

KAS. Let the record reflect… that I do not wish to fashion a weapon out of the ways I've had a shit time! Or do or say things because I'm a 'man of colour' – a title, by the way, I never agreed to. I mustn't have been on the right WhatsApp group when that was decided.

He glares at ADAEGO.

That doesn't make me a 'respectable immigrant'. It makes me a human being who wants to speak personally about my personal experience. I think that makes me a very disruptive immigrant, actually.

He looks at ADAEGO, *who goes to speak.*

I'm not taking questions – unless the question is 'red or white'?

That reminds him to top up his glass.

Look, sitting on the fence isn't as comfortable as you think. All of you sit in your armchairs of certainty – and they look much more comfortable to be honest. Not being sure about how you feel about every single thing seems to mean everyone hates you now. So let me climb off this plank of wood sticking up my arse and say… Jacq. Yes. I see you and I see why this is such a fucking dilemma for you. You were much poorer than I was growing up – and both of us were in a different league to Ethical Edgar and My Little Pony.

He indicates TOBIN *and* ADAEGO. *She rolls her eyes.*

ADAEGO. Okay. I did dressage for *one term* at school.

KAS (*furious*). Jacq was physically hungry at times when she was growing up.

ADAEGO *looks a bit shocked by this.* JACQ*'s embarrassed.*

Yeah – there was nothing 'at the table' at all sometimes.

He looks ADAEGO *in the eye.*

And, Adaego, there are times when having more melanin in your skin is a whole 'nother level. I'm sorry your beautiful face signifies a million complicated things to the people you pass in the street. I am. And yeah – I have obviously been 'randomly' searched at airports. Held up a stag do for four hours once. It's dehumanising. Sometimes the system can be fatal for people like you and me.

(*To the room.*) And even with all that – we here, us, are some of the very luckiest people who are alive now – or have ever lived. Or will probably ever live! We pay to go to a special room to run! We plug in a machine and burn fossil fuels to run nowhere so our hearts don't stop beating from all the

convenience and luxury we're swaddled in. We are in this blip
in history and geography – of 'vegan tacos and one-night
stands delivered to the door' – while the sea level rises –
and all we do is argue about who has the worst deckchair on
the *Titanic*.

He looks around at them.

And none of us do – by a long shot! Most people in the
world are living right now in grim, hard hardship –

ADAEGO. Yeah well, that's why I fight – for Black women
who live in hardship! Because they're my people –

KAS. Are they? Because as far I can see you spend most of
your time getting white women onto the right WhatsApp
groups.

She gasps in fury. TOBIN *ducks on* KAS's *behalf.* JACQ
freezes.

ADAEGO. Don't you dare judge me! It's not my job to solve
racism! And I do do stuff for disenfranchised women! I go
the extra mile.

KAS *nods furiously and squats on the counter.*

KAS. Oh yeah – you'll always go the extra mile, as long as it's
in first class. With a sex-shower.

JACQ *and* TOBIN *look at each other: Yikes.*

ADAEGO (*almost in tears*). I raise money for shelters! I've
volunteered with Eritrean refugees! I do a lot more than you!

KAS. I'm sure you do! But none of the arguments I've heard here
tonight have been about anyone outside this room. All I can
see is elite people using fancy academic language as shield
words – fighting about who's got the moral authority to speak
on behalf of those they'll never even share a sandwich with.

*There's a long silence as they recognise the truth of what he's
saying.*

ADAEGO. So what are you doing to change the world?

KAS. Not enough. But I'm not advertising I am. I'm not arguing from a high horse and pretending that's helping!

TOBIN. Hear hear!

KAS. – Seriously, mate, now. Fuck the fuck off.

KAS squares up to TOBIN.

TOBIN. Excuse me?

KAS. With all due respect – which is none at this point – if you had to do some kind of manual labour every day to stay white and straight and male and posh and… gender-conforming –

He turns to ADAEGO.

Yeah, I know fancy language too, thank you.

He turns back to TOBIN.

And… not disabled and to have the right to a passport… If you had to dig ditches in community service for all these meaningless nonsense markers that mean so much to the people who make decisions… the things that you were gifted at birth that open so many doors… Honestly – how long before you'd be a… brown lesbian? Tuesday?

TOBIN. No. I'd work for it – I'd dig ditches – because I appreciate that a certain amount of unfairness is built into the system –

KAS (*suddenly sober-seeming*). – Great. Well now you have an opportunity to show us that. That's what being dubbed a 'straight white posh man' is. That's what having assumptions that you might be 'one of those men' is. It's having to work to prove otherwise. Having to demonstrate the stereotypes about you aren't true – which you've failed to do tonight – spectacularly! We're just used to it!

TOBIN. Forgive me but –

KAS. No. I do not forgive you.

JACQ is turned on by this side of KAS.

JACQ. Kas.

KAS. And the truth is none of you would forgive me – if you knew.

JACQ. Knew what?

KAS. Knew what I did. And I have to carry it like some kind of dirty secret because you've all decided you're right and you're... honestly – so immovable now. Even though I've got *nothing* to apologise for.

ADAEGO. What did you do?

KAS. It's what I didn't do.

TOBIN. What didn't you do?

KAS stares at them in defiance.

KAS. Never have I ever... voted Remain.

They all flip out.

| JACQ. What the fuck? | TOBIN. What?! | ADAEGO. Jesus Christ?! |

And then a silence. A stronger reaction to this than TOBIN's offer of half a million quid. The three of them move and stand together against him.

JACQ. Get out!

JACQ points to the door. KAS laughs. He steps back up on his ladder to get away from them.

KAS. I didn't vote Leave either. I didn't vote.

TOBIN. Well that's worse. You just let it happen. You didn't even believe in anything.

ADAEGO. Another time you thought, 'Oh I shouldn't have a vote.' Amazing.

JACQ. I feel like I don't even know you.

ADAEGO. You hung us all out to dry because you were too gutless to pick a side.

JACQ *squats on the floor in the fetal position.*

JACQ. Kas. No. You're the reason courgettes cost a pound fifty. You're the reason we're going bankrupt.

TOBIN. It's a lot more complicated than that, Jacq, but, Kas, yes, you're a factor in your own bankruptcy.

JACQ *springs up and turns on* KAS *viciously.*

JACQ. And now you've made me agree with this prick.

KAS *sits on the stepladder, tired. Head in hands.*

Your father was an immigrant. He must be rolling in his grave –

KAS. – Hah! My dad would've voted Leave for sure. Hated the European Union.

JACQ*'s aghast: Nooo.*

Yes Jacq! 'We've' all got different opinions just like white people.

JACQ. I know that. I guess my family just… agrees on politics –

KAS. – Jacq. Your mum came on the Black Lives Matter march and clutched her handbag under her arm for dear life the whole time.

ADAEGO *laughs.* JACQ *makes a 'fair enough' face.* KAS *stares at them, mystified.*

None of you have asked me why.

They look at him. Shit. That's true.

You've all just shouted assumptions at me. You're not curious. You're not interested in understanding. This is your whole problem.

JACQ. So… why?

KAS (*sarcastic*). Well, thanks for asking, Jacq. Do you really actually want to know?

JACQ. Yes. I do.

KAS. I wanted to stay in the EU –

ADAEGO (*sarcastic*). If only there was some way you could've –

KAS. – LET ME SPEAK!... But, I just hated all the tribal 'Leave and Remain' bullshit so much! I didn't want any part of it. And, Jacq – do you understand how toxic it is that I couldn't express that to my partner because of these fixed ideological positions? You all think you're intellectuals but you buy into an off-the-rack way of thinking and it's one-size-fits-all. Well it doesn't fit *me*. Am I an amenable brown man now? Am I weak now?

He glares at ADAEGO *and* TOBIN. JACQ *softens*.

JACQ. I'm sorry, Kas...

KAS. My dad always said the irony of being an immigrant was that you had to keep your head down to keep it above water.

JACQ looks at him.

Sometimes it's just the only way I can cope with it all. Of course, if a bunch of rabid racists come to my door with sticks, I'll fight them. But I'm not fighting you. The people who are meant to be on my side. I won't. If we can't even build a bridge to each other, how the fuck are we going to build a bridge to people on the right? At very least we have to stop burning the bridges we already have. We just have to. We have to.

ADAEGO. So if you have the answers, tell us.

KAS. I don't have the answers. And neither do you. Or you. Or you. But we do. Together. We must do. Our communities do, if we'd just listen to each other and figure out what we do agree on and start there. All I know is this – we will never, ever be able to organise and build coalitions that make any fucking difference if we can't even talk to the people we love. And that... is the end of my TED Talk. Please feel free to kill each other now. Or – surprise me and don't.

He bows and jumps to the floor. They all sit with what he's said for a while. ADAEGO *pours* KAS *a wine.*

ADAEGO. Sometimes, it's just hard to see them as bridges. Sometimes, it just feels more like – being handcuffed to cunts.

KAS *turns to* JACQ.

KAS. Jacq – if we do go bankrupt – we'll move in with your mum and get new jobs and we'll be fine in a few years. We don't need you to do this.

JACQ. Of course we don't. And I won't.

ADAEGO. See! She doesn't want it, Tobin.

TOBIN. Six hundred thousand.

The room stops. Damn.

JACQ. I do want it.

A roar goes up.

BUT – wanting money isn't the same as being prepared to lose everything else. Unlike you, Tobin, I know when to stop.

TOBIN. But why should you stop at having two of us when you can collect the whole set? Fill up your loyalty card? Go on…

KAS *lunges forward and pushes* TOBIN *in the chest.* JACQ *quickly inserts herself between the two men to stop a fight. But* TOBIN *has no interest in entering a fight he's not convinced he'll win. He looks* JACQ *in the eye –*

Six hundred and *fifty* thousand pounds. Off the table altogether very soon.

KAS *steps towards* TOBIN *again, hands out –*

KAS. Just stop!

TOBIN *sees red.*

TOBIN. And did you stop, Kas? When you were fucking my wife? Did you think for one second to stop when you were repeatedly putting your penis into her –

He points to ADAEGO.

Or were you too busy 'building a bridge' from one of these women to the other?!

JACQ. Okay now.

KAS. You need to calm all the way down, man.

TOBIN. Don't tell me what I need to do. You've milked me for a hundred and twenty-*five* grand – and then had the gall to serve up a Château Pontet-Canet, as if you were announcing directors' dividends!

KAS (*muttering*). Jacq! I told you!

TOBIN. And then it turns out you've milked me for over a decade of marriage. What else do you want? Another line of my cocaine? My forgiveness? My Ducati? Nobody –

He spins around pointing.

– is to drink!

The others are all shocked.

Time to decide, Jacq. You can live with your mother for three years on a zero-hours contract. Never really get ahead. Or you can have over half a million choices. Six hundred and fifty thousand to be exact. Which is it to be?

JACQ *looks at* ADAEGO *and* KAS *and back at* TOBIN.

KAS (*to* JACQ). Do not let him pressure you. Do what *you* want.

ADAEGO. Kas. Can I see you outside, please?

The fire shoots up and the lights come down. Ruth Roubelle's 'Seven Nation Army' blares until the lights come up again.

When the music snaps off we see ADAEGO *and* KAS *lit up through the glass outside the restaurant.*

Inside the restaurant TOBIN*'s on his phone and* JACQ *busies herself away from him.*

I'm gonna go.

KAS. What? Now?

ADAEGO. You were right. It needs to be Jacq's decision and she won't be able to make it properly if I'm here.

KAS. Why? I thought you were dead against it.

ADAEGO. Yeah. Well obviously I hope she decides not to.

KAS. I think she will.

ADAEGO. But, what you said, about her being hungry as a kid... I didn't know that. And Tobin and I are over and out anyway, right?

KAS. What are you going to do now?

ADAEGO. For the first time in my life, I've got no idea. Check into a hotel tonight. Tomorrow...

She shrugs.

Kas. A lot of things have been said tonight. By me and by you.

KAS *nods.*

KAS. I'm sorry for what I –

ADAEGO. – No apologies. Just... if I call you tomorrow. Or next week. Or next year. Will you be there for me?

KAS. What do you mean?

ADAEGO. I mean will you pick up if I call? Because... I don't know who else I can talk to about what's happened here. Ever... And I might need... I'll be there for you, anyway.

KAS. Good. Because I normally talk to my mum about stuff and this will be difficult to explain.

She laughs a bit, tearfully.

I'll be there... Always.

They grab each other by the hand.

ADAEGO. I'm really sorry about all of this. He's punishing me at the end of us. And I really hope it doesn't mean the end of you two.

KAS. No apologies. But honestly, he's not after my relationship with Jacq. He's after your relationship with Jacq. That's the one he wants to destroy.

ADAEGO stops and takes a beat.

ADAEGO. You think?

KAS. Yes. And frankly, it's checkmate. It doesn't matter what she does now. She takes the money and you can never see her again. She doesn't take the money and you're… paying for lunch. Forever. So how many lunches do you think there'll be?

ADAEGO looks at him. He's right.

He destroyed your friendship the second he made the offer. He's clever.

Something in ADAEGO bubbles up.

ADAEGO. Fuck him. You're right. Fuck him.

The fire shoots up and the lights come down. 'Seven Nation Army' blares until the lights come up again.

ADAEGO and KAS talk in an animated way through the window but we can't hear them any more.

In the restaurant –

JACQ fidgets. TOBIN looks up from his phone.

TOBIN. Shall I go?

JACQ turns around.

JACQ. Do what you want?

TOBIN. If you'd told me to go, I'd have gone by now. What's stopping you?

JACQ *turns away and sips a drink.*

Is it that when I walk out the door, the cash goes with me?

JACQ *ignores him.*

Or is it that there's always been a little spark between us?

JACQ. What?

TOBIN. You used to wonder if I was naked under my coat.

JACQ. Not in a good way.

TOBIN. Hmmmmmmmmm.

JACQ. What?

TOBIN. Just… the way you're always bickering with me? Why is that?

JACQ. Oh you think our arguing is the beginning of some Hugh Grant film? Contempt isn't always foreplay, you know.

TOBIN. But sometimes it is.

JACQ. Why are you saying this?

TOBIN. Because I think you're going to say yes. And I need there to be… a spark.

JACQ (*Jesus God*). A spark?

TOBIN (*softly*). We're old friends, Jacq. There's always a possibility… with old friends… isn't there? A moment that could've been more…

JACQ. Stop doing that thing.

TOBIN. What thing?

JACQ. The thing with your voice. Where you talk more softly so I have to lean in to hear you.

TOBIN (*almost whispering*). And that's the moment.

The flame hops high in the air – and JACQ *and* TOBIN *are plunged into darkness. 'Seven Nation Army' blares.*

The lights go down and the fire goes up in the restaurant. When the lights come up again, the boys are outside – as far away from each other as possible. ADAEGO *is inside, up close to* JACQ. *The music snaps off.*

ADAEGO (*shouting*). I know you're going to do it! You made up your mind the second he suggested it!

JACQ. If you don't even trust me then why am I even not doing it!!?

ADAEGO (*softly*). We haven't got long!

JACQ. What?

ADAEGO (*softly*). You have to look angry. Like we are having a fight.

JACQ (*softly*). What? We are having a fight, aren't we?

ADAEGO (*softly*). I think you should take the money.

JACQ. Adaego. What? Why?

ADAEGO (*quietly*). Look angry! Shout.

(*Loudly.*) Fuck you!

JACQ (*going along with it*). Fuck you!

ADAEGO (*quietly but with an urgent voice and a pretend angry face and some cross gestures*). Kas said you and I are fucked if we do and fucked if we don't now. He's right.

JACQ. But –

ADAEGO. Look angrier! It's got to look like a fight.

JACQ (*loudly*). I can't believe you're saying this! How dare you?!

ADAEGO (*softly*). You were right. My marriage is over anyway. Was in some ways… always a sham. I think we're all fucked whatever happens now, so you might as well be not be fucked and poor.

JACQ (*softly*). But if I walk away, at least he doesn't get what he wants.

ADAEGO. Hah! You think this is what he wants?

(*For* TOBIN*'s benefit*.) AFTER EVERYTHING WE'VE BEEN THROUGH!

JACQ (*to her*). Isn't it?

(*For show*.) Whatever!

ADAEGO (*quietly*). You can go down on someone for a lot less than half a mill. Honestly… he doesn't even like doing it.

JACQ. What?! But on your hen night you said… he was thorough.

ADAEGO. I didn't, did I? Did I? Well he *is* a high-achiever. But it's not his favourite thing and honestly, I know he can't afford it. He's fucking himself over to spite us.

ADAEGO *looks at the door, worried.*

(*Loudly*.) Not this bisexual thing *again*?!

JACQ (*loudly*). Oh shut up and go then!

(*Softly*.) I can't because… Even if I lose you, I'll know I didn't lose respect for myself.

ADAEGO *puts her hands on her face and searches for a way out…*

ADAEGO. Okay. What about… if we take him together… like a… heist?

JACQ. A heist?

ADAEGO. Shhhhhhh. Is this nuts?

JACQ. Lol. Yes. Obviously. Crackers.

ADAEGO. Maybe. I don't know. But it's the one thing he won't be expecting. For us to team up. Say 'Time's Up' in the weirdest possible way.

JACQ. The weirdest possible way! Okay. Maybe. But... I could only do this on one condition.

ADAEGO. HOW DARE YOU!?

JACQ. OH I DARE! If it really is a heist we've gotta split the money fifty-fifty.

You and me.

ADAEGO *shakes her head – adamant.*

ADAEGO. No, I don't need it.

JACQ. Whaddayamean? You're a single woman tomorrow and a freelance feminist journalist!

ADAEGO. Oh shit.

JACQ. Welcome to how the other half live. Beyond our means.

ADAEGO. Fuck. You're right... But no because I'll get a divorce settlement.

JACQ. Do you want him to give you something? Or do you want to take something from him?

ADAEGO *loves this idea and takes a beat to enjoy it.*

ADAEGO. Oh I really do... But not half. When you're doing all... the work.

JACQ. What else was it you said on that podcast?... 'They don't call it emotional *labour* for nothing.'

ADAEGO *smiles.* JACQ*'s an excellent negotiator but...*

I can only agree to it if you take half.

In that case... ADAEGO *puts out her hand low under the counter to shake* JACQ*'s in secret.*

(For show.) ARE YOU INSANE?!

(For real.) Are you absolutely sure?

ADAEGO. NEVER BEEN SANER! We're building a bridge. A bridge he'll never expect us to build.

JACQ *secretly shakes*.

JACQ (*quietly*). Yes.

(*Loudly.*) You're going too far!

ADAEGO. Are we an army?

JACQ (*for real*). We are.

(*For show.*) Anything else you need to get off your chest?!

ADAEGO (*quietly*). Yes. He'll try to back out of it. Ask for coke. That'll get him to do some more. Remind him that he made a 'gentleman's agreement' – use that phrase – that means something to him. I'll go. I'll come back for you. He won't split us up.

(*Loudly.*) I hate you!

(*Softly.*) I love you.

JACQ (*loudly*). I FEEL EXACTLY THE SAME WAY.

(*Softly.*) I really do…

ADAEGO. I'm gonna storm off.

She looks back and whispers –

Oh and if you push the right buttons I reckon he'll go up to seven hundred and fifty.

JACQ. What are the right buttons?

ADAEGO. Tell him it has to be eight so you seem like the compromiser when he comes down.

JACQ nods. ADAEGO grabs her bag. She opens the door. TOBIN and KAS come in.

Well, I tried to stop this. For all your sakes. I can't be any part of it. And imagine I won't be seeing any of you again. Good luck to you all.

She throws her bag over her shoulder.

(*To KAS and JACQ.*) Don't let him ride that fucking bike. He's high. He could kill someone.

She snatches his keys up off the counter in case, walks out and slams the door. The three of them sit together for a while. Silent. Fuck. This is it. But what is it?

TOBIN. So!

JACQ. So…

KAS. So?

JACQ. What happens now?

TOBIN. That's up to you, isn't it?

JACQ. We need a moment alone.

> TOBIN *nods. Goes on his phone.*

Could you?

She points to the cellar. He goes downstairs and she slides the manhole cover across. JACQ *goes far away from the hole and faces* KAS.

(*Quietly.*) Adaego is in.

KAS. So I gathered. But it's not her call.

JACQ. Well, it was something you said, so you've only got yourself to blame.

> KAS *laughs.*

KAS. As always.

JACQ. She wants to take him together. So, we can do this if we want. Or – we can totally not do this. Lock him in the cellar. Leave.

KAS. Okay. Let's do that.

JACQ. Or…

KAS (*sure*). Or…

JACQ. Adaego reckons he'll go to seven hundred and fifty thousand. The deal is we split it with her. Fifty-fifty. So he doesn't split us up.

KAS *takes a moment to take this in.*

Free money. We close this place down. Move to Cornwall.
Or Australia. Start a fish-and-chip shop. Get a flat. Get
married even. If you still want that.

KAS. I don't know.

JACQ (*suddenly remembering*). We could have shower-sex on
a plane!

KAS *laughs but it's hollow.*

I'm sick to death of having no choice. It's just a few
unpleasant minutes. Like a smear.

KAS. A smear?

JACQ. In exchange for hundreds of thousands of choices...

KAS *shakes his head.*

KAS. I don't know, Jacq. Wouldn't we always look back though
and –

JACQ. – No. We'd never look back again. Because we'd finally
have something to look forward to.

KAS. Okay. If that's what you really want. It's your body.

JACQ. But you've got to be in.

KAS. Jacq. If he wanted to suck my cock – I promise you'd get
zero say. I'd disable the comments.

JACQ *nods: Fair. True. They look at each other. A switch
flips. It suddenly goes fast and frenetic. Like they're in Vegas
or on a game show with sixty seconds to decide.*

JACQ. How will you feel after? If I do it?!

KAS. Real talk?!

JACQ. Real talk!

KAS (*faster*). I've got no fucking idea.

JACQ (*faster*). But if you had to guess.

KAS. How would you feel if he went down on me, babe?

JACQ. Lol. Super-confused. Don't know. Couldn't say.

KAS. I'm holding loads of cash. I'm zipping up my fly. How do you feel?

JACQ. Fuck!!

KAS. Weird game show, right?

JACQ. Fuck!!!!

KAS (*like a personal trainer, positive, but pushing her*). You're rolling the dice, babe. Whatcha gonna do?

Faster.

JACQ. I really fancy you like this, you know!

Faster.

KAS. Well, I'll bear that in mind.

JACQ. Can you?!

KAS. Babe. Time to decide. Yes. Or no.

She looks around. Over half a million quid. Fuck it.

JACQ. I don't want us to be poor and tired and overworked and blaming each other – I love you.

KAS (*faster*). I love you too. Whatever happens here. You're a fucking goddess!

JACQ (*punching the air*). I feel like one!

KAS (*pulling her to him*). Hey. No promises. Best efforts.

JACQ. I understand.

She pulls herself together. Gets her businesslike face on and bangs on the cellar manhole cover with a broom handle.
TOBIN *emerges.*

TOBIN. Yes?

JACQ. Here are the rules. This is a purchase. An acquisition. Not a merger. My right to commodify my body for my profit.

TOBIN. You're the boss.

JACQ looks at him suspiciously.

JACQ. Can you really transfer this much money in one go?

TOBIN. I can. There's a service called CHAPS –

KAS. Of course there is –

TOBIN. No, no... It stands for Clearing House Automated Payment –

KAS. – It stands for Cunts Have All the Power.

KAS is pleased with his quick thinking and sick with anticipation.

JACQ. Just set it up. I want it ready to press send or the deal is off.

TOBIN looks around to the chaos of the restaurant from the long night of drinking and partying.

TOBIN. Aren't we going to go to a hotel or something?

JACQ. No, mate. You've not bought the girlfriend experience.

TOBIN. I wasn't thinking of me. I was thinking of you.

JACQ. Too late for thinking of others, Tobin.

TOBIN. Well where are we going to do it?

JACQ. Here!

TOBIN. Here? In front of the window?!

JACQ. Well obviously we'll put the lights out.

TOBIN (*awkward*). Yes. That would be best.

She looks at him. Is he wavering?

JACQ. Do you not want to do this?

TOBIN. I'd be more comfortable doing it next week, I think. In a better location.

She leans closer to him.

JACQ (*evoking the spark*). Say that again. I didn't hear it –

TOBIN (*quieter*). Maybe in a week?

JACQ. Do you have any more coke?

He cuts her a line off the left-over coke on the table.

TOBIN. Er... yes... There's no rush, is there? Hotel? Do the bank transfer properly.

She does a line and so does he.

JACQ. Gentleman's agreement. Stays in the room. Money transferred tonight.

She rubs some coke into her gums and looks at him.

Gentleman's agreement.

TOBIN *pulls out his phone.*

Oh and I want eight hundred thousand.

TOBIN. No.

TOBIN *sees his way out of it.* JACQ *laughs.*

JACQ. Adaego said you wouldn't go through with it. That you're a coward.

TOBIN *sets his jaw.*

TOBIN. I'll go to seven hundred thousand. That's it.

JACQ *knows the plan is to come down to seven hundred and fifty but she suddenly doesn't want to.*

JACQ. I'm worth eight.

TOBIN. You're worth what someone will pay. And I'm the only someone offering.

KAS *steps forward.* JACQ *holds* KAS *off.*

JACQ (*to* TOBIN). I'm worth what I say I'm worth. I learned that from watching you work.

This is an ego boost to TOBIN, *who's feeling trapped and alone. He's flattered. He can't disagree with her or he loses his moment. He nods. She's got her money.* KAS *is strangely impressed by* JACQ's *skill.*

TOBIN (*to* JACQ). Put your account number and sort code in here –

JACQ gets out her debit card and puts the numbers in. TOBIN *looks at* KAS.

JACQ (*mutters*). CHAPSing the cash…

KAS (*kind of horrified*). They just let you move that much money around online –

TOBIN. – If you have premier banking privileges with Coutts.

KAS. 'Privileges' being the operative word.

TOBIN (*to* KAS). Are you going to leave?

KAS. No. I don't trust you.

KAS looks at JACQ.

I'll be here. Just shout 'stop' when you want to stop. I'll be here.

KAS turns his back. JACQ *climbs up onto the central counter with her back to the audience.*

TOBIN. Why don't you lie down at least?

JACQ. Get on your fucking knees.

She pushes him down by the shoulders and he disappears behind the counter – kneeling.

KAS kills the lights. In the shadows, the silhouette of JACQ *puts her hand on the button. A flame shoots up in the air as music blares.*

Only KAS *is lit. Back to the action facing the audience. Taking it for her. After a while –*

Stop!

KAS. That's enough. You heard her.

The music snaps off and the lights snap up.

You've had your pound of flesh. You got what you wanted. Leave her alone.

JACQ *shifts away.* KAS *pulls* TOBIN *up by the lapels. He's floppy, disoriented and drunk.* KAS *thinks about punching him and then releases him – as* JACQ *adjusts her clothes and climbs off the counter. She picks up his phone and hands it to him.*

JACQ. Do it now. I wanna watch.

TOBIN *does.* JACQ *stands over his shoulder and checks. He has. She looks him dead in the eye.*

Your wife was better.

TOBIN *laughs.*

TOBIN. She always will be.

KAS *holds* JACQ *by the hands.*

KAS. You alright?

TOBIN *flops on a stool and passes out on the counter.*

JACQ. Yep.

KAS. How do we feel?

JACQ. Dunno.

KAS. Relatable content.

JACQ (*searching*). Fish-and-chip shop or… plane-shower-sex? Or…?

They look at each other.

JACQ *sighs.*

KAS. Probably not this week.

JACQ. Whatcha gonna do then?

KAS. Fuck knows.

She looks scared. He wants to make her laugh.

I could just run off with Jacinta Allen.

JACQ *laughs despite herself.*

JACQ (*trying not to cry*). Damn. That was my plan.

He looks at her funny face.

KAS. I'm going to miss doing this. With you.

JACQ (*trying harder not to cry*). Me too.

KAS. I'm very fond of you. In a way.

JACQ. You really are one of the good ones…

She turns away. He grabs her hand.

KAS. There's a chance we might've just burned this bridge.

JACQ. We'll build a new one.

KAS. Deal.

They shake. A pact. They'll find their way back to each other. If they can.

JACQ *gets her bag. They head for the glass doors – and go through. Have a moment together outside. He walks off. She stands in the doorway.*

TOBIN *sits slumped over the counter in the quiet for a while.*

There's a roaring noise beyond the doors. He doesn't get up. JACQ *looks behind her, jumps back inside the restaurant and moves to one side.*

ADAEGO *smashes through the glass door on* TOBIN*'s motorbike and deliberately crashes the bike into a countertop.* TOBIN *turns around. She gets off the bike and drops it.* JACQ *stands well back but a hundred per cent behind her.*

TOBIN *faces her. They stand ten paces from each other. It's like high noon.*

ADAEGO. Just wanted to say, I've realised something tonight. I've stopped being a full person to you, a long time ago. I've become an embodiment of the last five years. It's not just my work that's an avatar to you, is it? Maybe in some ways I've always represented something to you. A million complicated things, I guess. And that's why you were capable of this. This cruelty today.

TOBIN *takes a breath to speak.*

– No! I'm talking now! You're listening! Why did you even want to marry a twenty-two-year-old, Tobin? Because you wanted to be a mentor for life. The thing you adored most about me was how I made you look and feel. You wanted someone in your kitchen, your car, your bed – looking up to you – impressed by you. Well, I'm not so impressed any more. Looking back – there were so many red flags when I met you, I could've made bunting!

TOBIN *thinks about speaking.*

This rage – it's because you're scared you're over. And I get it, because… it's a bit of a moot point… you are over. And it's not because you're white or a man. Some of my favourite David Attenboroughs are straight white men. It's because you were never doing any of this for the right reasons and you just can't shake the idea that power belongs to you. It is difficult for men right now. Without doubt.

He looks up at her, surprised at her giving a little ground.

It's difficult for all of us. Men are not used to sharing a little bit of their power. Women are not used to having a little bit of power. Maybe we are wielding it with a certain amount of… glee at times. It'll find a balance. And I am not giving myself a Get Out of Jail Free Card, Tobin. I have heard some things about myself tonight that were difficult to hear.

He looks at her – surprised.

The challenge now is to change. And I know I can do that. Because all my life I've had to bend and adapt to survive. To thrive. And honestly… I feel for you because we are living through a time of huge change and you've got no skills for that.

She points around the room. Like tonight.

You've been trained to do this. By your school. Your industry. By all the movies you've seen. Humility is a muscle. Adaptability is a skill. Owning vulnerability is hard won. And here you are in a time of great upheaval, living in a lava lamp, unable to bend and bounce. I hope you can find a way to learn. But honestly, it's not my problem any more. What you did tonight – you thought it would break me. That you could divide and conquer and break us apart.

She turns and looks at JACQ.

But we decided to stand together.

He looks at them: What?

We did this together. Fifty-fifty. Yeah. You underestimated our ability to bend at speed. Now, how much will you destroy before you change even a little bit. This…

She looks around the room at his carnage.

…has set me free. And now – I'm going to soar. We're going to soar. And you're going to have to watch.

He looks at her. And nods. A flicker of remorse or at least an acknowledgement. She turns around and throws the keys of the bike over her shoulder.

Oh and there's something wrong with your Ducati.

She passes the bike she wrecked, puts her arm around JACQ *who does the same – and they walk out of the restaurant together.*

TOBIN *walks forward with the whiskey bottle in hand – he relaxes his arm and accidentally spills some on the floor. He keeps walking (his back still to us) now deliberately spilling it in a trail through the restaurant. He drops his head and all four of the flames leap in the air at once in a whoosh.*

The lights snap to black.

www.nickhernbooks.co.uk

facebook.com/nickhernbooks

twitter.com/nickhernbooks